MASTERCLASS COLOURING

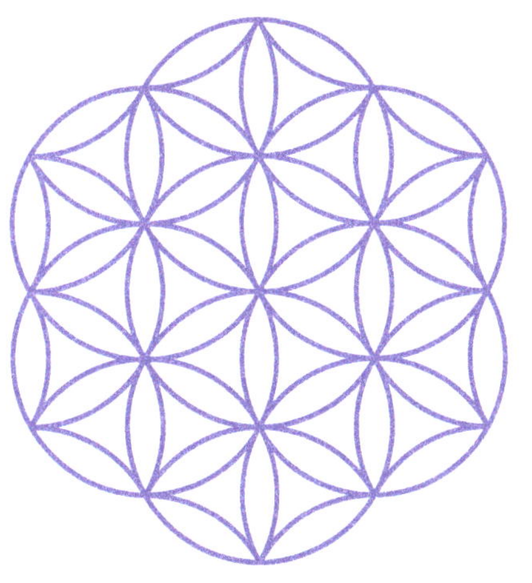

&DRAWING

The WORLD of NATURE

Written and Illustrated by
Greg C Grace

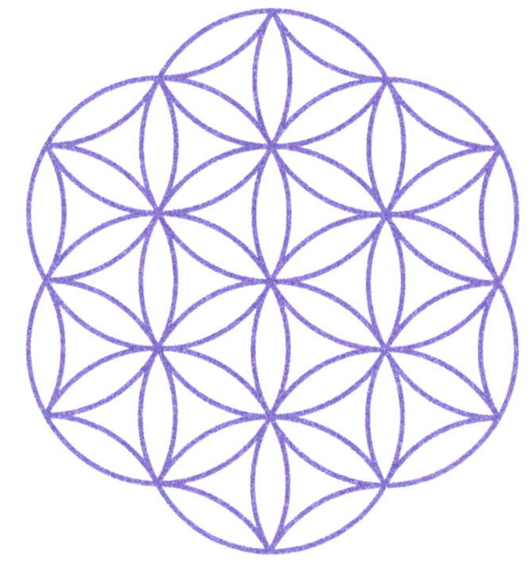

MASTERCLASS COLOURING & DRAWING

Written and Illustrated

by

Greg C Grace

ISBN:9780994461926

CONTENTS

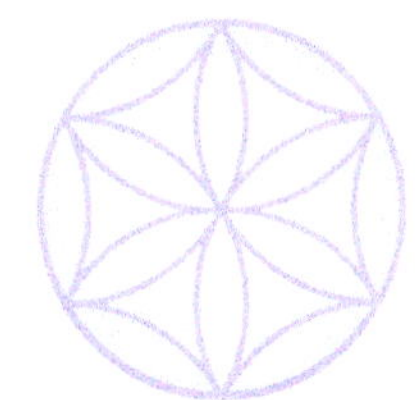

About the Author

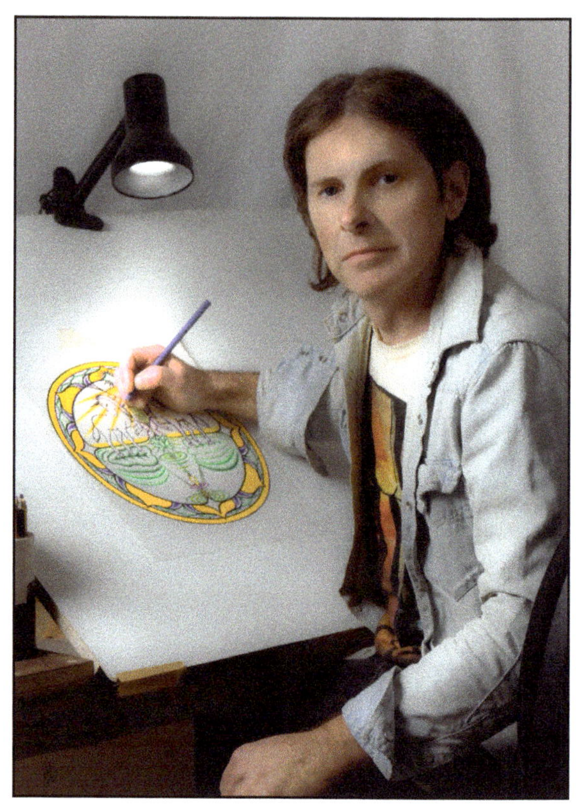

Greg C Grace is an innovative and visionary artist who lives in Adelaide, South Australia. He has spent more than 20 years within the wider artistic community, helping define the very boundaries of where consciousness and creativity meet.

Through his extensive studies, Greg has become an authority in the fields of Sacred Geometry, Transpersonal and Comparative Cosmology, Mandalas, and Dreamtime Art. He is also a renown Vedic Astrologer and personal Vastu consultant, practicing in these fields for over 15 years. His published works include over a dozen titles, covering fields such as colouring, drawing, graphic symbolism, gems and crystals, along with the creation of several interractive design series.

Greg has considerable experience in the fields of Jyotish, Ayurveda, Transpersonal Therapy, Chromotherapy (Colour Therapy) and Orthomolecular Nutrition. He is also an accomplished Nature & Wildlife Photographer, specialising in the fields of Native Birds, Gems and Minerals. Greg's vivid and Impactful images have been Published repeatedly the world over, such as 'BBC Wildlife Magazine' and 'The New York Post'. He has amassed one of the world's largest specialty stock libraries through his many gem photographic sessions over the past 15 years and through his travels around Australia and abroad.

With his inspirational techniques and vast store of creative wisdom, Greg has seen great success practicing as a Franchise, Branding and Self Development Consultant for the past 15 years. His clients have included many and varied Individuals, Organisations, Business Developers and Entrepreneurs throughout the world. His accumulated wisdom and boundless appreciation for all mediums of creativity have made him a sought out authority in the fields of Written and Visual Storytelling, Artistic Symbolism and Cross-cultural Cosmology.

Greg's comprehensive work as a Graphic Designer, Product and Project Developer has led to a broader and more user-friendly approach towards teaching, mentoring and the very conception of this 'Masterclass Series'. He hopes to continue his life journey of sharing this empowering wisdom and creative inspiration for many years to come.

Follow Greg C Grace:

www.gregcgracephotography.com or visit him on linkedin to access weblinks, stock libraries, portfolio, published works/titles, work history and current and future projects.

~ This Book is dedicated to my late father ***Rick Grace***, who showed much love and appreciation for the world of nature - the ocean, animals, plants, birds and trees. Some of my fondest memories were spent with dad in his gardens and bird avearies, along with the many trips to coastal and country locations. Diving for abalone with him as a boy, outback motorcyle trips, riding with dad and my two brothers, or time spent basking in the sun with mum and dad at the beach and in our family garden at Valley View, South Australia ~

Introduction

The Colouring and Drawing Masterclass Series was developed for both beginner and advanced colouring enthusiasts alike. It offers various colouring masterclasses and drawing techniques, with a focus on awakening creativity and latent artistic talent. This impactful new series of colouring and drawing products are designed to help enliven inspiration and creative journeying. The artwork styles are varied, employing Cross-cultural Symbolism, Mandalas and Animal Totems, along with Sacred Geometry, Steroegraphic Imagery and nature patterns from the plant kingdom.

The techniques contained within utilise colour as a medium for general mental and emotional wellbeing. They are also suited for therapeutic and transpersonal applications. Working with Mandalas and Stereographic Imagery for example, has been found to bring equilibrium between the left and right hemispheres of the brain. With a concentrative focus, greater mental relaxation and a deeper sense of harmony is attained within. In a world where our inner sense of peace and balance is constantly being challenged by the oscillation and drama of modern day living, artistic pastimes and practices that help achieve greater tranquility and mental wellbeing become welcome assets indeed.

The Nature designs and colouring styles contained in this book were produced over may months and all artwork was produced by hand. Even though rulers and compasses are suggested at the front of the book, all circles and arches here were conceived freehand. Likewise with straight lines, they are all done by hand. Rulers are useful as a measuring device and to define or sketch out segments or regions, yet if rulers and compasses are used to ink or pencil in final markings the design can lose its dynamic appeal or become less vibrantly alive. Artwork that is stereographic and almost identically symmetrical from left to right, yet slightly off a perfect mirror, has been shown to have restorative and potential remedial effects on the mind of the viewer. Geometric copying with slight variation is the key to many life forms and genetic replication in Nature. However if every creative form was an exact copy or clone of another, the world would become pretty bland and tiresome indeed.

The artistic techniques employed are designed with a balance of Geometry, Stereographic mirroring and more random free-flowing designs or motifs from Mother Nature. Some are more suited to tattoo style designs or glyphs, with dynamic styling and bolder lines, whereas some are more open and full-page with thinner line segments. However, there is generally a lower threshold set on line density, as the designs are all hand drawn with ink pens. The lines are sketched up to a certain thickness or density of black. Artwork of this detail takes much longer to produce with many designs taking well over a day's work to complete. Many colouring books on the market may become difficult or tiresome when the lines are too thin to colour segments effortlessly in between. This can create frustration, the exact thing colouring pastimes otherwise aim to remedy or reduce.

Images with dynamic designs and thicker lines may be suited for bold colours and ink pens, with pencils more suited to the general body of the book. Shading and colour gradients are often best achieved with pencil, yet feel free to mix both mediums, or mix pencils with watercolour pencils. Experiment too with soft and hard pencils, as each give their own effect of colour saturation. So choose which best suits your inclinations and artistic style. The whole point is to get lost in the journey, have fun or at least some time out. For when time is not counted or measured on our creative journey we find that artistic application becomes more innate, meditative or 'freeing' to the spirit. This is the essence of what artistic endeavours are really all about, to awaken our creative spark, our essential nature, our sense or insight and vision. To become fully awake creatively is what it takes for the human mind to thrive — and through awakening creativity we become more inspired, more fully alive.

Things You May Need

To complete the exercises in this book you will need some simple art supplies. Most of these are inexpensive, easy to obtain and include basic equipment such as pencils, eraser, ink pens, transparent ruler, compass and paper. As you become confident with your drawing skills there is no end to the creative ways you can colour your designs. Your local art supplier will be able to advise you on the available range of quality paper and colouring pencils, markers and paints.

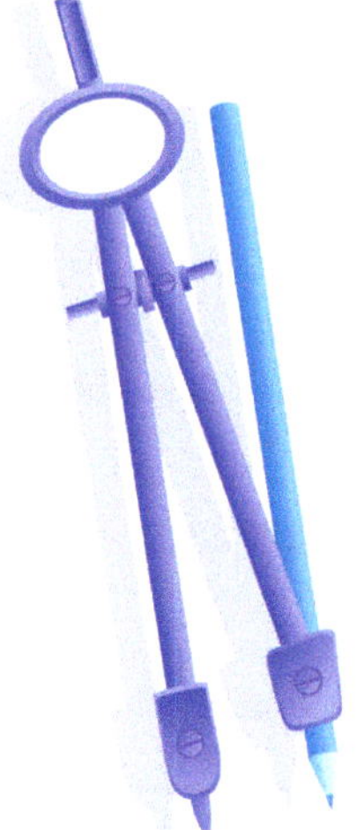

Compass: Useful for drawing circles and aligning curved shapes. Look for one which allows you to change the pencil and thereby incorporate coloured pencils and markers.

Eraser: a good quality soft white eraser is preferable as it will help keep paper clean.

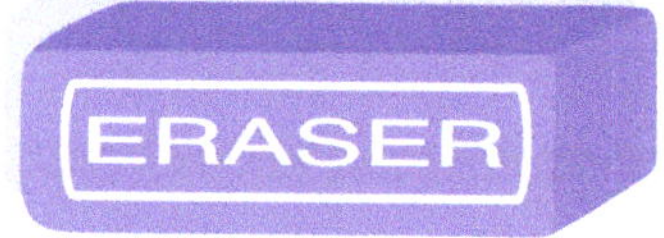

Ruler: for drawing straight lines and making accurate measurements. A transparent plastic ruler is most effective as it allows you to align your measurements with other shapes.

Paper: for practise and drawing similar designs, clean white A4 size sheets of bond paper are ideal; however for a better finish you may wish to use a quality art paper. The paper for colouring panels in this book is left blank on the back side so that there is little or no show-through on your final completed artworks.

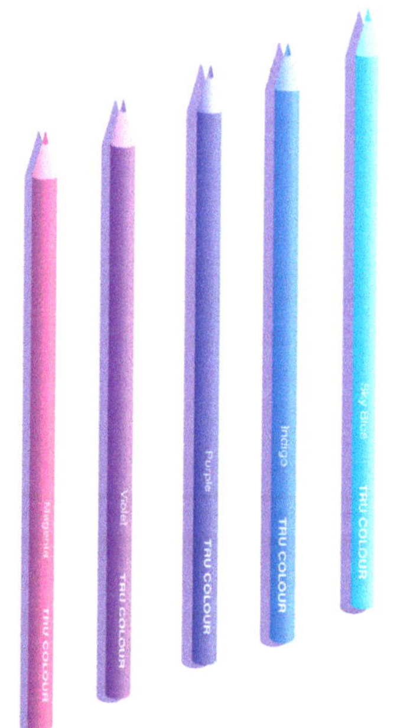

Pencils: for colouring and drawing your designs, including guidelines and outlines. Graphite pencils are preferred, particularly the HB grade as this is neither too dark nor light and can be easily erased. Coloured pencils are ideal for defining and colouring your finished designs. Harder art quality pencils are better for defining lines and edges while soft pencils are preferable for a smooth finish.

Pens: for inking your designs. Ink pens come in a variety of styles and size tips. The bulk of the images in this book were done with a common black pen or 'biro'. Some fine line pigment ink pens are useful for fine lines and circle work. It is often best to experiment with many pens styles and then choose the ones you are more comfortable with. Even coloured ink pens can be used for some styles and again, experiment with ink pens in terms of thickness and colour density.

How to Use This Book

The ***Masterclass Colouring and Drawing Series*** has been designed using traditional freehand drawing methods. These 'innovative' classes are aimed at awakening your artistic potential through the creative use of colouring lines, shapes, symbols, mandalas and geometry. Although this is fundamentally a colouring book, drawing insights and techniques have been added to highlight the symbolic qualities of different shapes and images, along with how to stylise your graphic artworks.

General Drawing Tips

For each exercise A4 size paper is recommended, or provided in the case of the colouring panels. Although, once you feel confident designs can be created to any size. Drawing at a larger scale simply requires allowances to be added for the proportions being copied or measured. For any of the exercises that utilise colour, simply follow the instructions, which in most cases use the paper and designs provided.

When drawing new shapes and symbols you might like to practise on a separate sheet of paper until pleased with the result. This can save unnecessary pencil lines and erasing. Using a separate sheet also allows you to trace your image a number of times until you are confident when drawing more spontaneously. This is particularly important where repetition and symmetry is needed.

If you have trouble seeing through the paper when tracing images hold it against a window, or using an active computer screen or device may help. Yes, tracing is an acceptable and useful drawing skill in the beginning when defining or memorising certain unfamiliar form outlines.

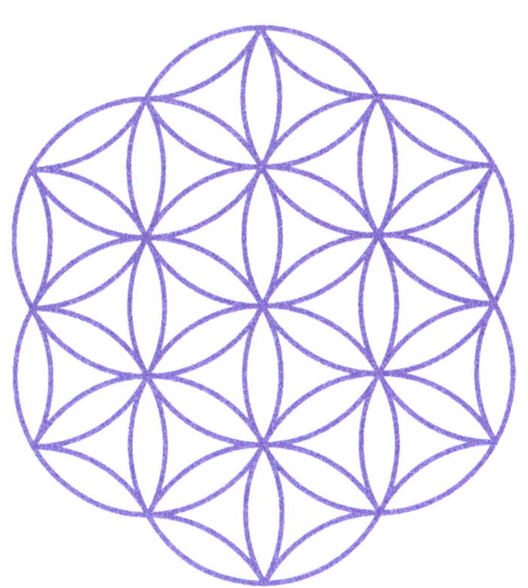

Keep pencil guidelines clear, yet light, as when the designs are inked you will carefully erase them. To highlight and colour your finished artwork you may use coloured pencils for a soft look, or art-quality pens or markers for a more defined finish. Gouache (for rich colour), or acrylic paint (ideal for larger designs) may even be used, or any combination which suits. Experiment freely with each for different effects.

Drawing Outlines, Circles and Squares

Drawing circles and squares with a ruler or compass is the most accurate and precise method. However, most of the colouring designs in this book were composed freehand. This is an art in itself and can often be learnt by first tracing some of the circles or curved designs in pencil and then detailing in ink by hand once you have sharpened up the pencil lines by drawing and erasing a few times. This is a great skill to learn and 'practice makes perfect' is not entirely the aim, as designs can often be a little 'asymmetrical' to help keep an organic or 'hand drawn' feel.

Using What You Learn

The information and exercises in this book lay the foundation for learning to draw and colour designs and graphic art panels. While these are guidelines to help you create symbolically rich designs, there are no firm rules. There is no end to the wide range of designs you can create, neither is there a limit to colour application practices, mediums or choices. Part of learning how to better colour and draw is using your imagination and trusting yourself, even if this requires latent or previously unused talent surfacing or awakening in the process. More than anything the experience should be enjoyable. Allow yourself to be open to experimentation in the process of becoming more creatively alive.

Masterclass 1: Understanding and Creating Colour Wheels

Many general theories and models are available on the use of the colour wheel. Some represent a basic or superficial understanding of colour. Others may present a colour model from a limited perspective or personal bias, without explaining the core qualities or practical value of individual colours. Study the colour wheels and supporting text within this book and come to your own conclusions as to how you can best utilise colour in your artwork and personal colouring experience. No one model is right or wrong and to avoid getting bogged down in lofty colour theory, let's look at some fundamental basics of the colour wheel geared towards practical application. Also, feel free to consult the colour qualities section in 'Masterclass 8' and 'Masterclass 9' for further information and experimentation on your colouring journey.

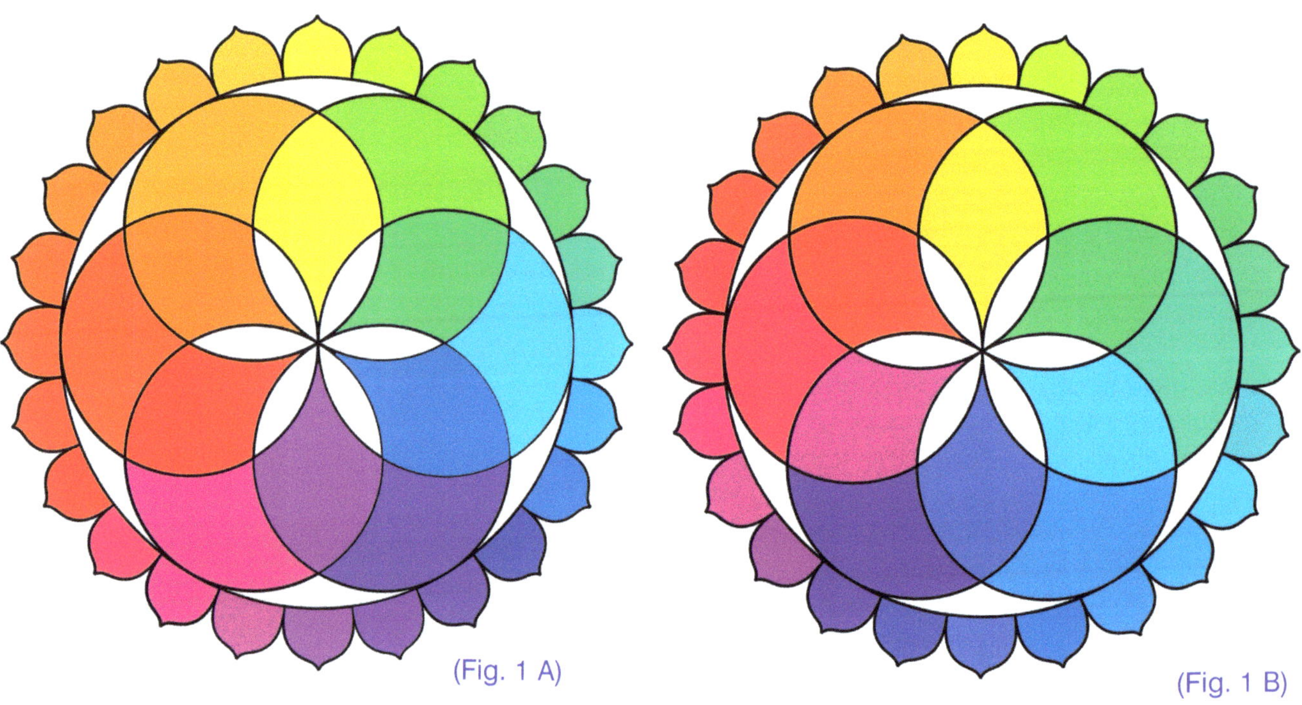

(Fig. 1 A)

(Fig. 1 B)

Colour wheel (Fig. 1 A) is constructed from six base complementary opposites and forms the basis of many colour models. It works through how colours impact the psyche and mind, and to how human vision interracts with colours in the natural world. The complementary opposite of hot-red is cool green, like we see in traffic lights. For example, staring at a hot-red triangle on a white card for some time, then immediately looking to a blank white card, we will see a colour-opposite green version of the same image for a short period. This is due to a sympathetic resonance and equilibrium being attained of the principles of how we process colour through the eyes at a core level.

The centre six petals of the colour wheel (Fig. 1 B) is constructed from two sets of primary colours: (1) 'Subtractive Primaries' (Cyan, Yellow and Magenta) used for inks, pigments and paints in the art and print trade. (2) 'Additive Primaries' (Red, Green and Blue) for digital colour monitors, photography and admixtures of coloured or additive light. If we put the two together to form the base six hues of the (Fig. 1 B) colour wheel, they work fine for the utilisation of distinct colour hues up to the twelve-point colour wheel. However, as we expand beyond the twelve in equal measure and progress to a twenty-four point colour wheel, there starts to become neighbouring colours which are a bit too similar and not distinct steps from one hue to another. This is most evident in an over-abundance of the red and green colour hues, at the expense of, or minimal representation of, the gold-orange and violet/purple hues.

Likewise, with (Fig. 1A) - as we expand into the twentyfour-point wheel, we see the opposite to Fig.1B, with similarities existing here in the orange and violet/purple bands, with a limited representation of the cool green and red-violet hues. Neither offer a balanced outer wheel, still (Fig. 1B) is the closest to ideal for a twentyfour point colour wheel in terms of a distinct step progression of colours or hues.

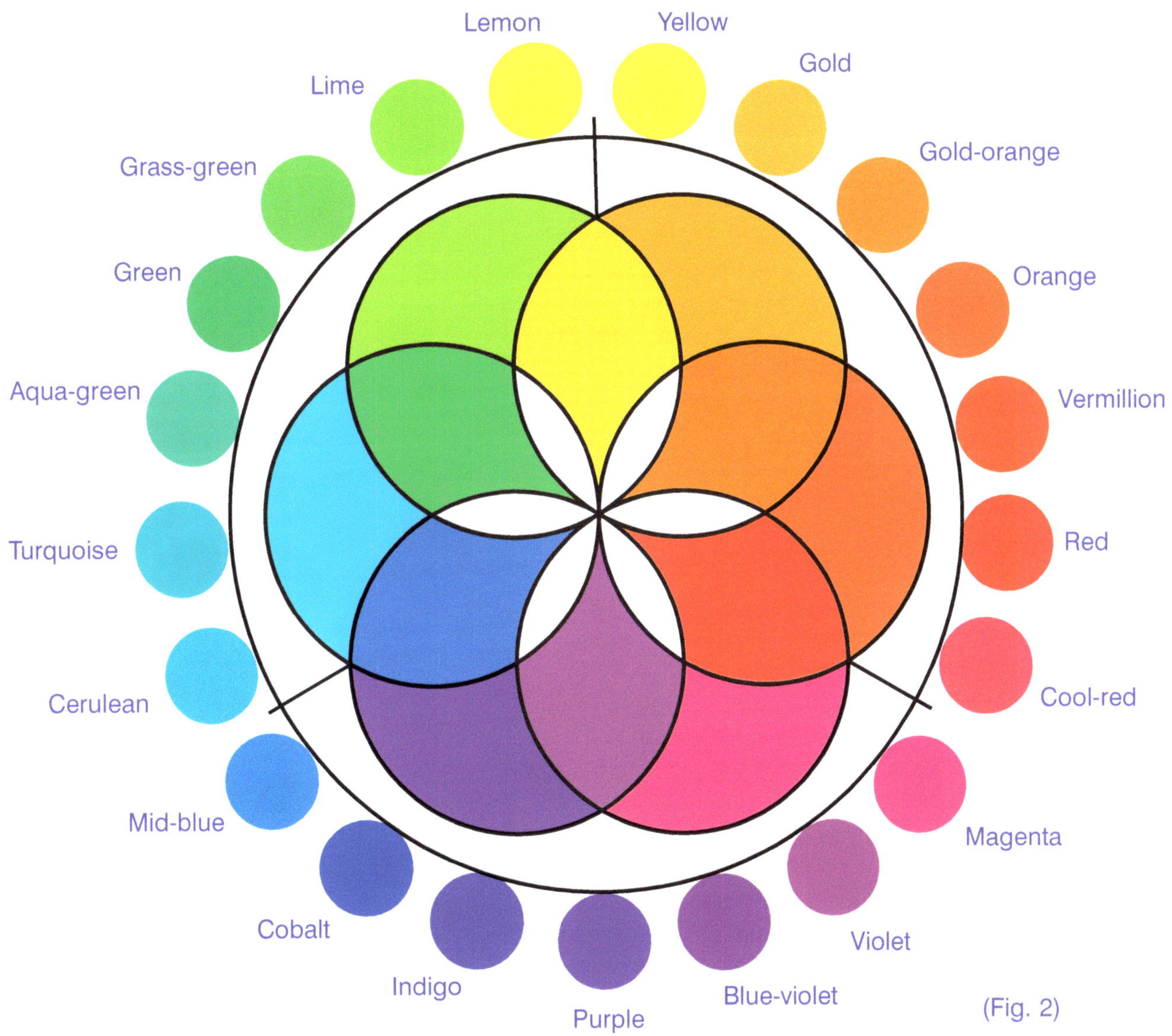

(Fig. 2)

It is easy to introduce limitations at the very core level of colour wheel construction. We may risk creating a 'less than ideal' colour progression at the outer-most expansion of the colour wheel. We may also produce a colour wheel unsuitable for effective colouring and creating well defined artworks. If colours chosen to be used next to each other in artwork are too similar, even by two steps on the colour wheel, the image can lose visual impact or vibrancy. With this in mind, the ideal colour wheel seems to exist around the 'twenty-one point' colour phase in terms of practical colour definition. Beyond this the human eye starts to lose its sense of defined boundaries in terms of what might be considered a distinct step in hue progression. These twenty-one hue values (Fig.2) are named for convenience sake and in support of the practical step progressional model. It is important however to not get too caught up in the names, as we each have a different understanding of colour on account of our mental conditioning and learnt association between colour as a subject and our experiences in the outer world.

So study the various colour wheels and dive deep into the medium of colour to create you art pieces. Be prepared to doubt and question what you once thought to be a known boundary in your knowledge and application of colour. In studying colour theory and colour models a bit of confusion is a good thing, as it fosters a deeper inquiry into the multifaceted potential of the many diverse and wonderful hues of nature. For any one hue is merely a snapshot or partial solidification of light rays, either suspended in matter by the application of a paint or pigment, or given off and accentuated as reflected light. We are just lucky on our colouring journey that we can fix defined boundaries and bold representations of colour through the use of inks, pencils and paints. Alternatively, we may seek a more fluid or open expression of the subtle nuances of colour in its capacity to provide variations of lighter or soft pastel hues.

Masterclass 2: Choosing Colours For a Nature Mandala - Defining Complementary Colour Qualities and Effects

Complementary colours can be categorised into two pairs of dynamics: (A) 'Complementary opposites' and (B) 'Supportive Complementaries'. Thirdly, there are 'Conflictual Colours' that may be imposing on, or that do not rest well with one another, causing an uncomplementary effect. They create a sense of alarm and may even give rise to feelings of aversion or sickliness when put together with no other supporting colours. Complementary opposites are the ones in the centre six of the colour wheel (Fig. 1A), which shows the opposites, like we see in the red and green of traffic lights. Supportive complementaries are very useful and dynamic in colouring panels, artwork and designs, as they help bring out the best aspects of another colour and 'complement' the other. A fourth category is one in which a third colour is added to augment or shift the focus on two conflictual colours, achieving balance overall, yet this is a subject for further exploration. See 'Masterclass 9' for further use of complementary colours.

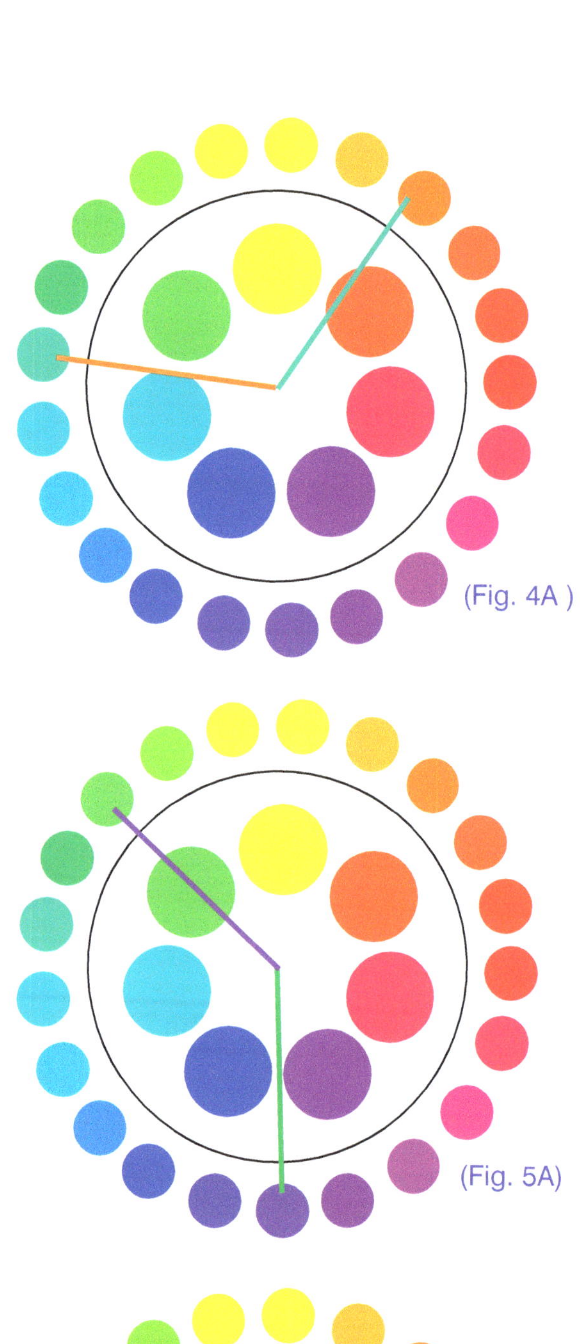

(Fig. 4A)

(Fig. 5A)

This exercise focuses on two colours, with the chosen mandala relating to the crab totem and zodiac sign of Cancer. The mandala relates to the fifteen day cycle from New to Full Moon and depicts feminine energies of creation associated with the very ebb and flow or flux of the life force. *The five mandalas in this masterclass were all coloured by hand with pencils to A3 size.

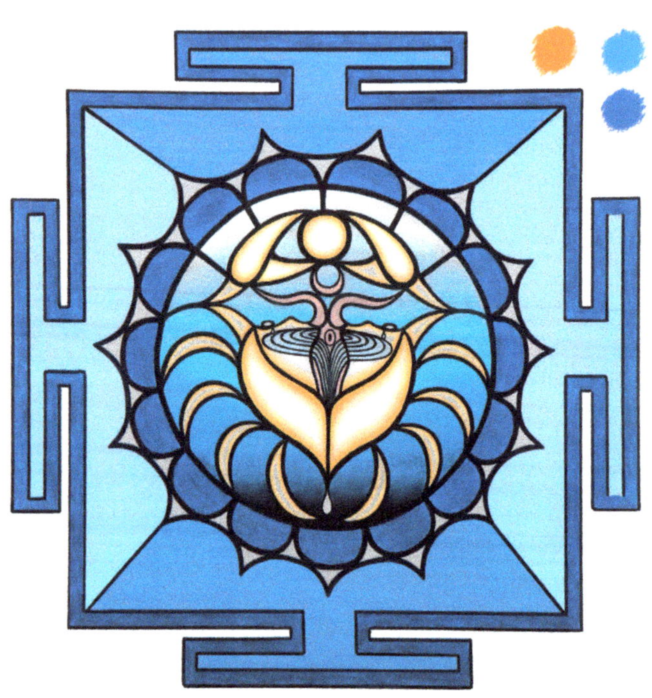

*Direct Complementary opposites and colours that relate to the Crab totem

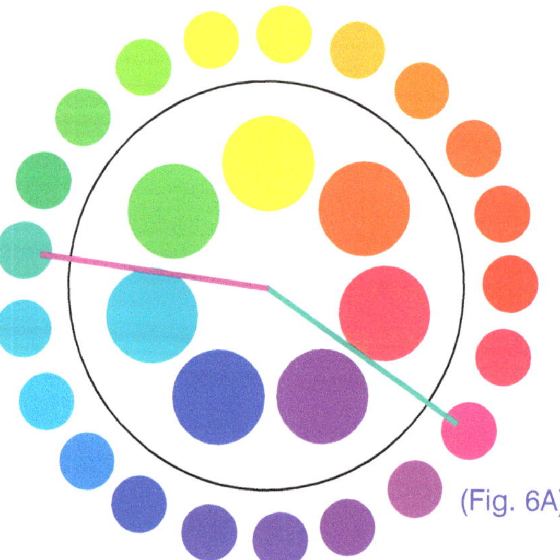

(Fig. 6A)

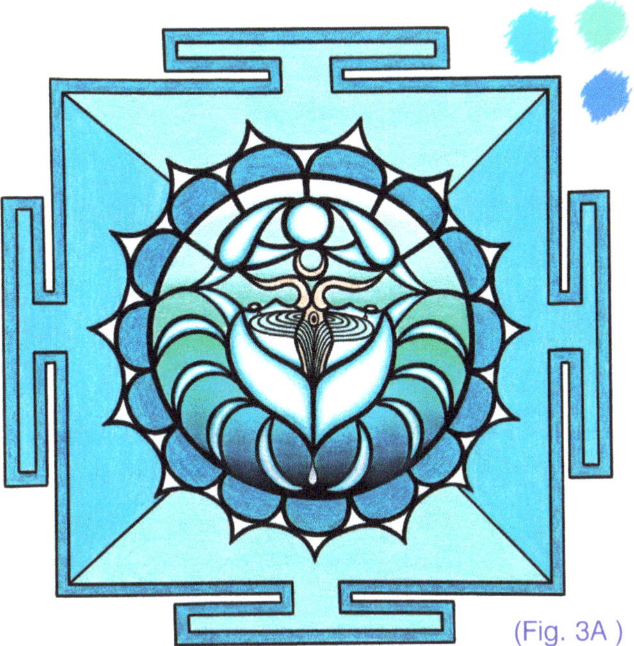

(Fig. 3A)

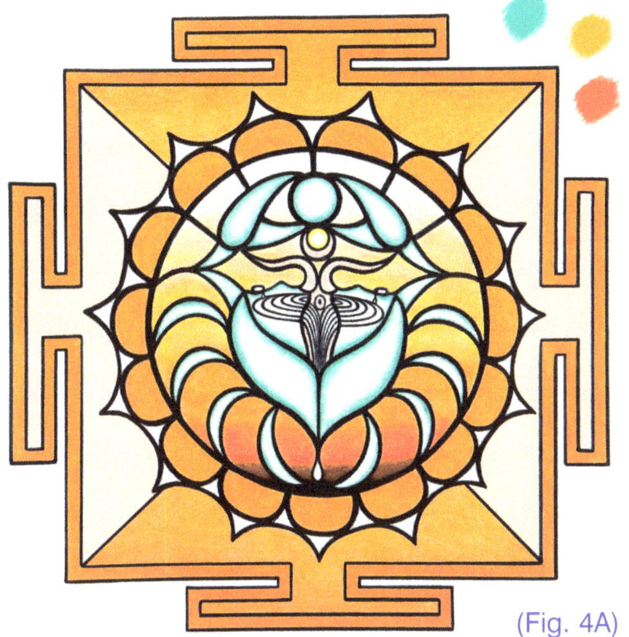

(Fig. 4A)

Colours chosen above utilise blue/aqua colours for water environment and the crab. These hues are adjacent hues on the colour wheel, as the pure cyan or sky blue mixes and merges with the turquoise and aqua green hues. The final image is relaxing and has a peaceful quality about it. The peachy flesh tones, being the only other element of colour in the design. When saturated these peachy tones become a complementary opposite of orange.

The orange and golden tones matched with a rich aqua green above are more dynamic. Aqua is six steps anti-clockwise on the colour wheel from the golden orange hues. This design is more vibrantly alive with the golden-orange hues relating to the crab totem and the aqua greens relating to the sea-greens of nature. Supportive complementaries in this case, which are one step away from complementary opposites of green and red.

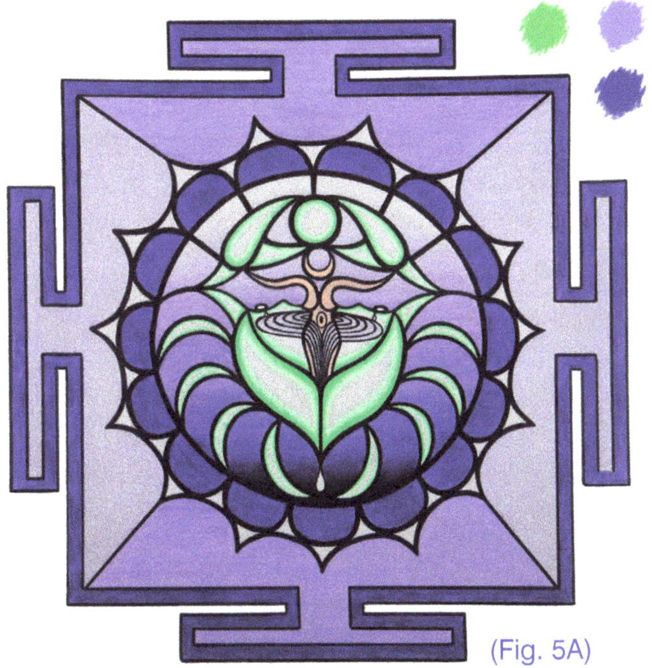

(Fig. 5A)

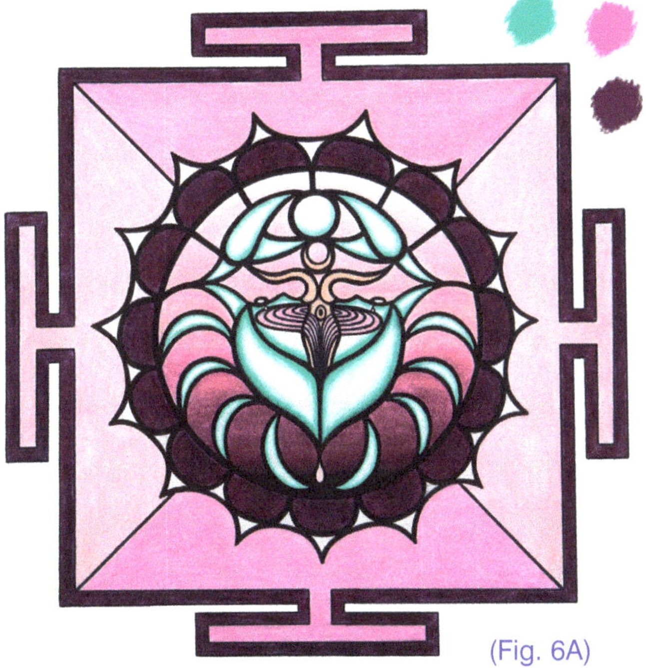

(Fig. 6A)

Complementary opposites are here shifted toward each other on the colour wheel, with grass green matched with deep purple. This green is slightly warm and the purple slightly cool, together creating balance. This shows graphically the effect of supportive complementary opposites, with the resulting effect representing balance and invigoration to the psyche, even if the colours do not relate to the natural depiction of the image, the crab totem, or the zodiac sign of Cancer.

This last example utilises a similar aqua center, yet this time gives a deep burgundy as the complementary hue. This burgundy hue is actually a deep red-violet or magenta on the colour wheel, which is 12 steps clockwise on the outer rim of the wheel. The effectiveness of this design in terms of complimentary colours is achieved by the fact that it takes complimentary opposites of red and green and moves them around a step or toward each other on the colour wheel.

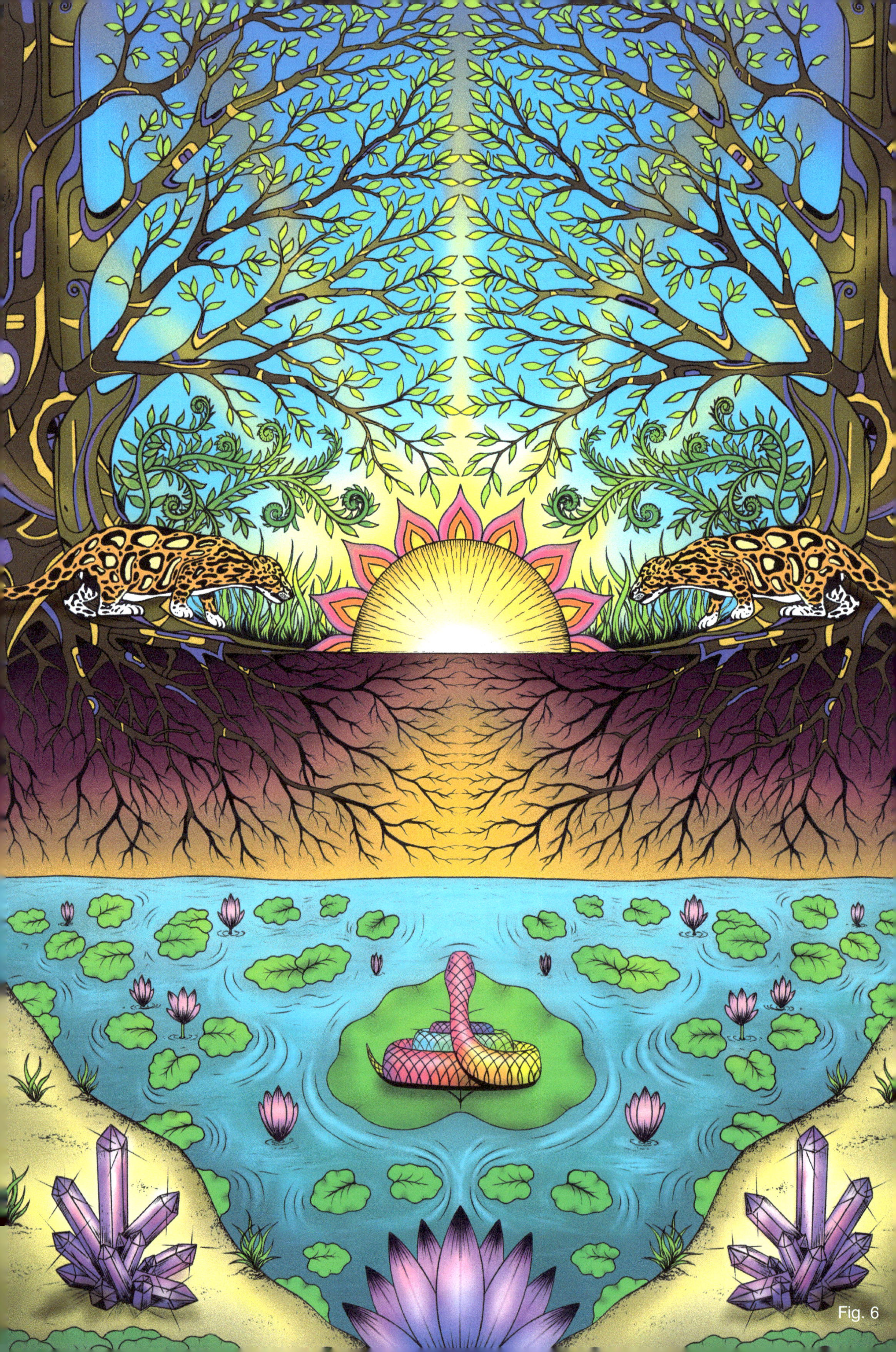

Fig. 6

Masterclass 3: Examining Colour Choice for the Colour Panels

Suncats (Fig. 6) - Forest cats, in this case 'the jaguar', are associated with totemic qualities of integrity and personal power. They represent refined sensitivity to the radiating light of the sun and life giving principle of nature. Cats can be coloured as lions, leopards or jaguars with camouflaged markings. The main colour effect here is the orange of the jaguars with the complementary blue hues. Added to this we have the contrasting greens and earthy brown which bring cohesiveness to the design. The deep burgundy is also a hue associated with the integration of emotional intensity and personal power.

Forest Wren (Fig. 8) - This colour panel is created in light of the spring call of the forest wren. To match the wren's qualities, bold, vibrant and effervescent colours were chosen and to match twilight the sky in spring. The image was started with the colourful blue wren, which was then accented with aqua and gold markings for emphasis and variegation. The tree was painted in dusty pinks to mirror dusk or twilight. The flowers and fruits were then added last to compliment and bring balance once other colours are set in. The sky was exaggerated to include both warmth and neutrality with the variety of hues, which helped the overall image become more vibrantly alive.

Dolphin hawk (Fig. 9) - This stylised graphic design is in the tattoo style and has been coloured relative to the animal totem's surroundings. Stylised water elements for the manta ray at bottom relates to the indigo, blue and aqua hues. The best way to colour this panel and avoid clashing colours was to colour a section or element of the design with the next adjacent element or section in mind. So the indigo, blue and aqua colours for the bottom half of the image were alternated, with colour being built up to create a balancing and pleasing effect. Likewise with the top section, where colours for the earth and sun were chosen to compliment the indigo and aqua hues below.

Oasis (Fig.10) - This ocean setting relates well to the blue and aqua tones. Complementary tones to these, such as yellows and oranges worked well with some image elements, along with bright magenta and violets for corals and fish. Green was chosen to be complementary in its emerald and lime hues. The undersea world is great to explore with a multitude of colouring options at your disposal. Base blue hues such as indigo, electric blue and aqua bring a bold and dynamic contrast to the warmer hues associated with the Sun, such as golds, orange, red and magenta. There are endless options for colouring corals, anemones, marine fish, crabs and turtles, and these were drawn on to depict the very potential diversity of nature's colour palette.

Australian Birds (Fig. 11) - Parrots have an intricate connection to passion and love in folklore and cultural traditions. Colour choice here is what would ideally take place in their natural surroundings with nature-identical colour choices for the parrots. One thing with Australian parrots is that they are given to colour mutation, which is evident in the pink bourke parrot at bottom left of the right-hand page. Here I chose a pink bourke parrot for the female. The rest of the birds were coloured in their full spring colours, or in similar pencil shadings that would be most vibrant to work with the black and white outlines. The sky was coloured and toned last to finally set the overall mood of the panel.

Cranes (Fig. 12) - This panel was coloured in balancing indigo blue, aqua blue and green. The lotus flowers represent new life emerging so were coloured with complementary bright yellows and soft pinks. The Crane totem resonates to the Indigo (wisdom and insight) and blue/aqua (perseverance and support) hues, so these were chosen to be prominent in the body of the colouring. Indigo is an odd choice for water, yet it was chosen here to help define and to complement what might otherwise be a light or soft looking image. The orange magnolias symbolise nurturing and enduring love. The indigo and earthy bark colours give the image more weight and add an element of depth and earthiness.

Hummingbirds (Fig. 13) - Hummingbirds relate to the principle of joy and the energies of spring. Colours chosen are variegated hues with minimal dark colours and the avoidance of red. A balance of soft pinks and pastel rainbow colours were chosen to complement the feather and flower elements. Magenta or hot-pink can be chosen in place of red in images where red would not suit the totemic value or aesthetic appeal of the image. Warm and mid violets also are useful in this regard. Alternatively, many alternate complimentary opposite hue variations could be chosen from the colour qualities section.

Colouring Example for A Nature Mandalas

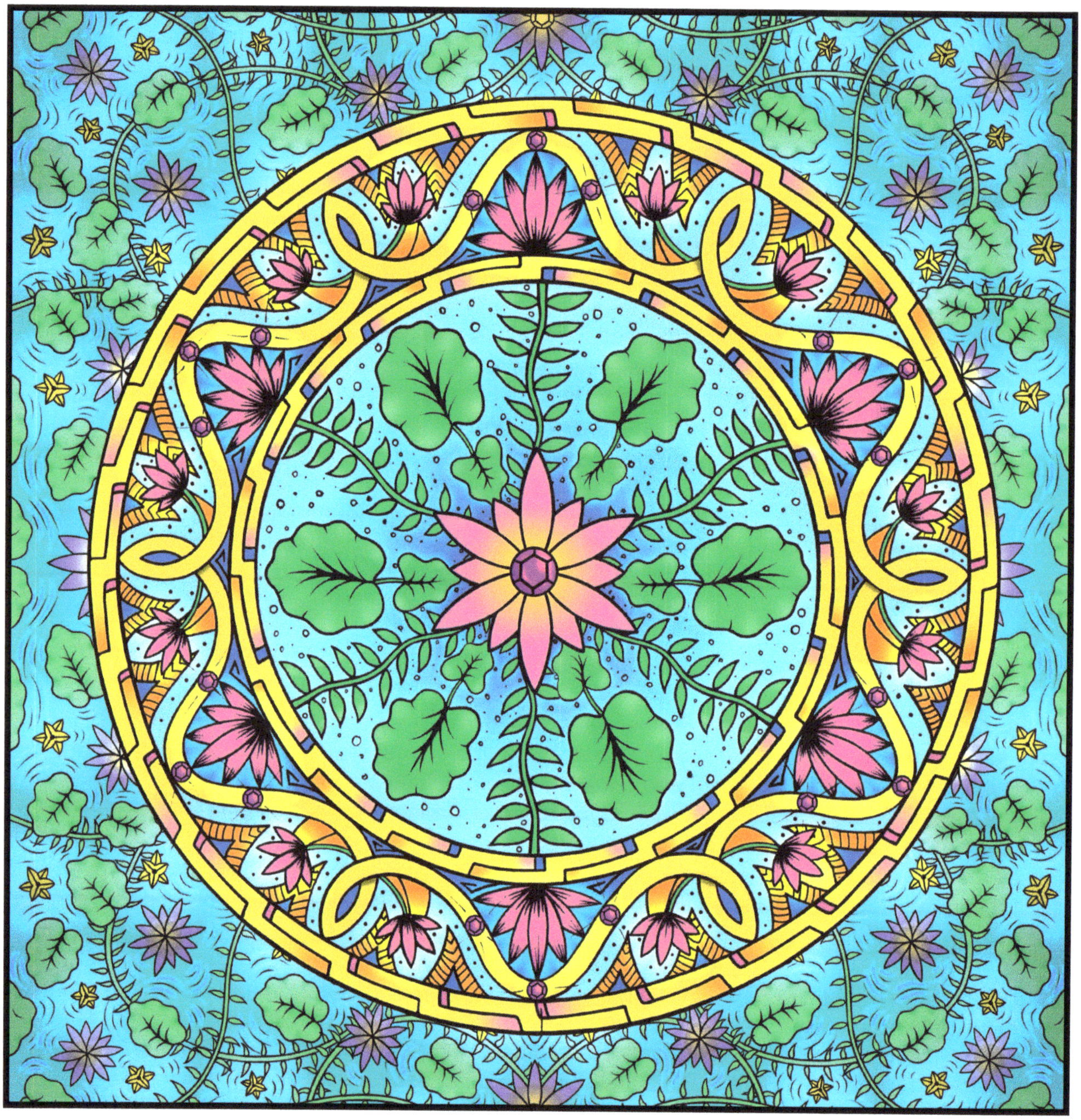

Fig. 7

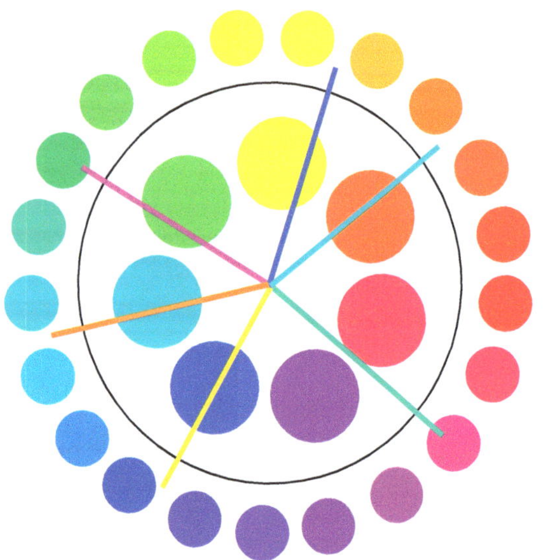

The above nature mandala is coloured in groups of complementary opposites which become balancing yet visually arresting at the same time. The proces of conceptualising the colours for this panel was to first start with the obvious nature-identical colours of green for the lotus leaves and blue for the water. From there we brought in the principle of supportive complementaries and complementary opposites, adding indigo for emphasis and matching with opposite golden-yellow hues. Touches of orange bring dynamic emphasis to the cyan or aqua blue tones. Pink violet or light magenta was matched with its opposite of cool green. You will see that some complementaries are not directly opposite on the colour wheel and this is often the key for creating dynamic colour effects and visually appeasing effects.

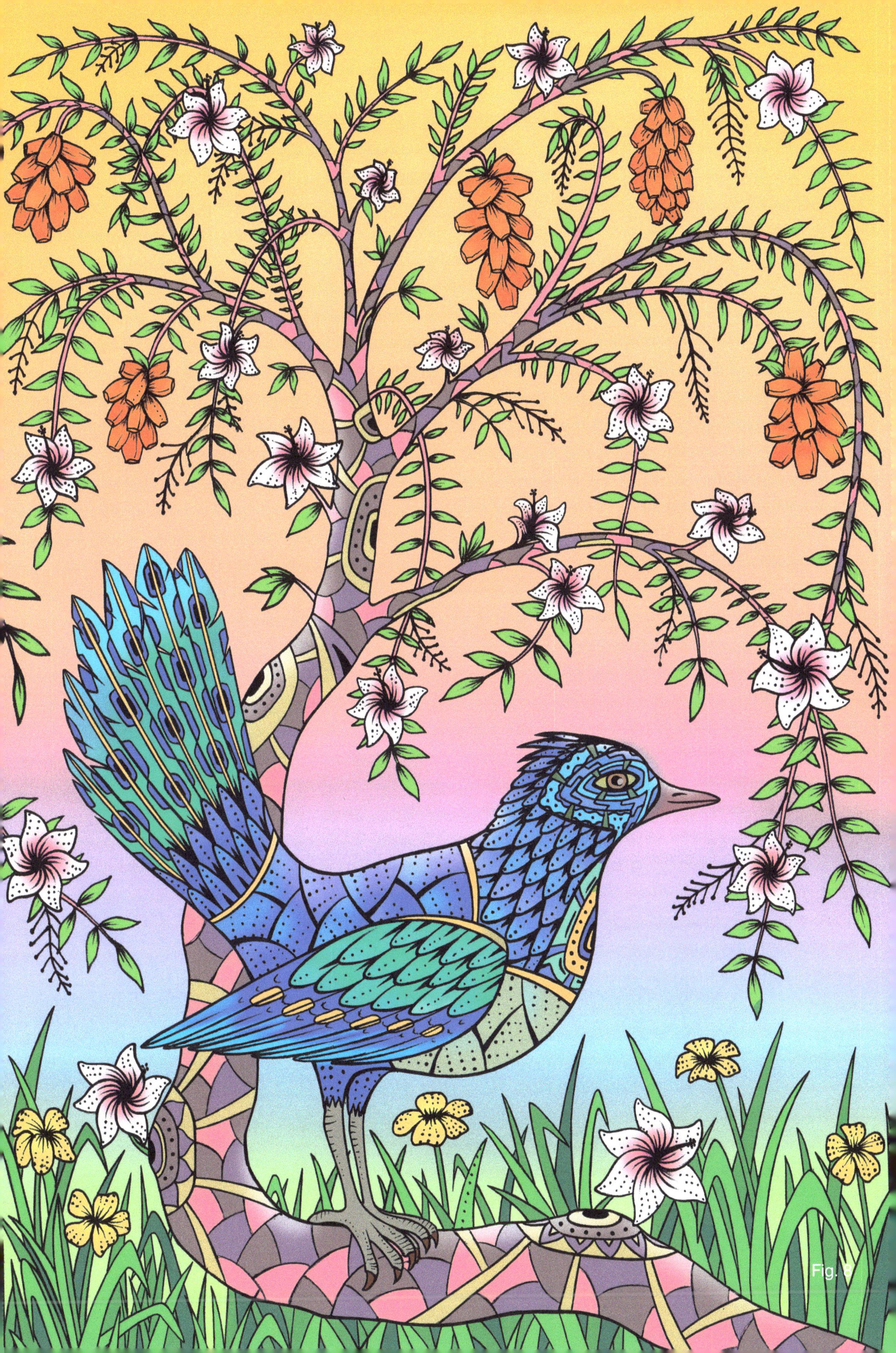
Fig. 8

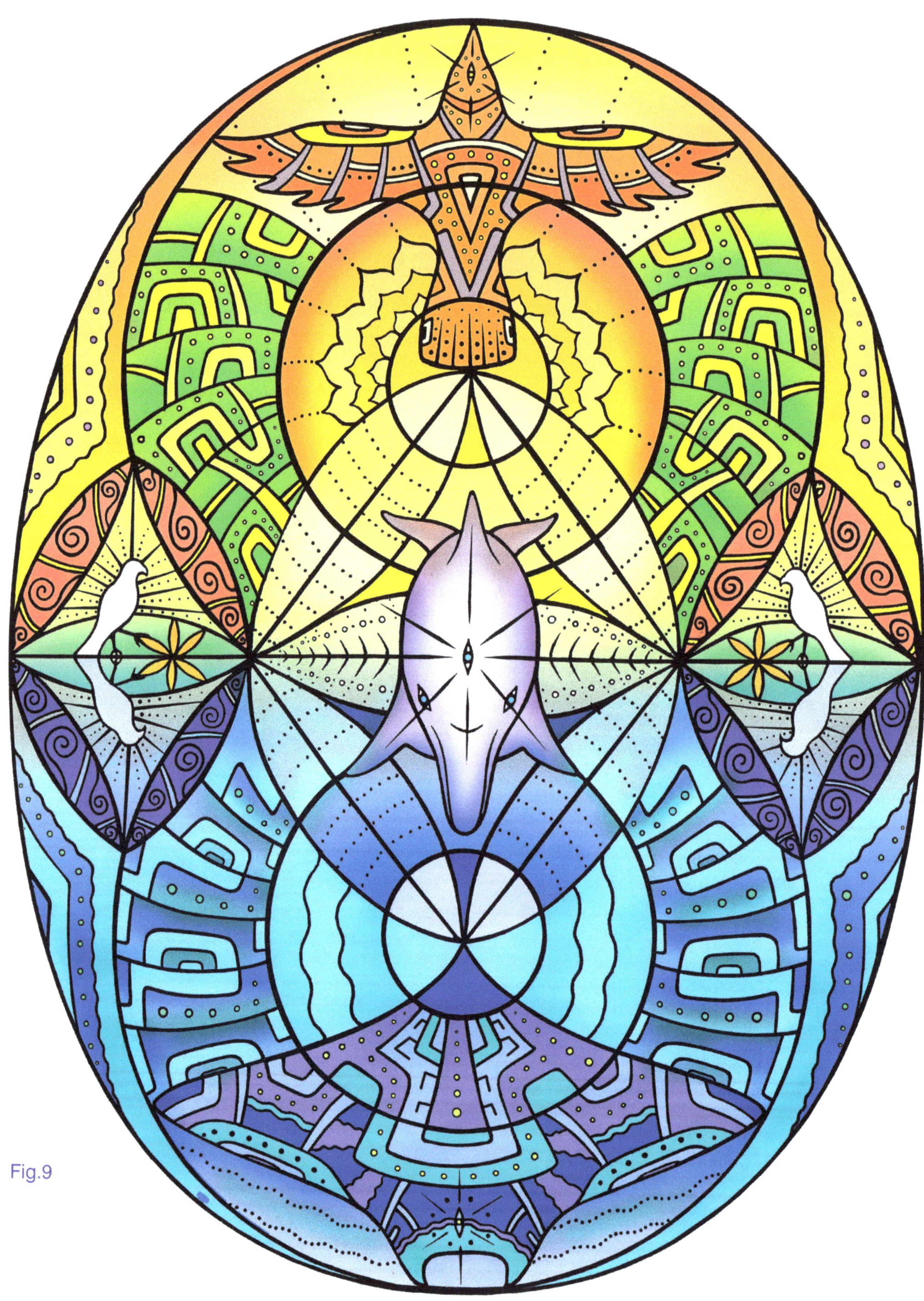

Fig.9

This graphic design is more suited to transpersonal art or tatoo-type stylisation. On the opposite page we have dolphins, yet in a more interactive colouring panel.

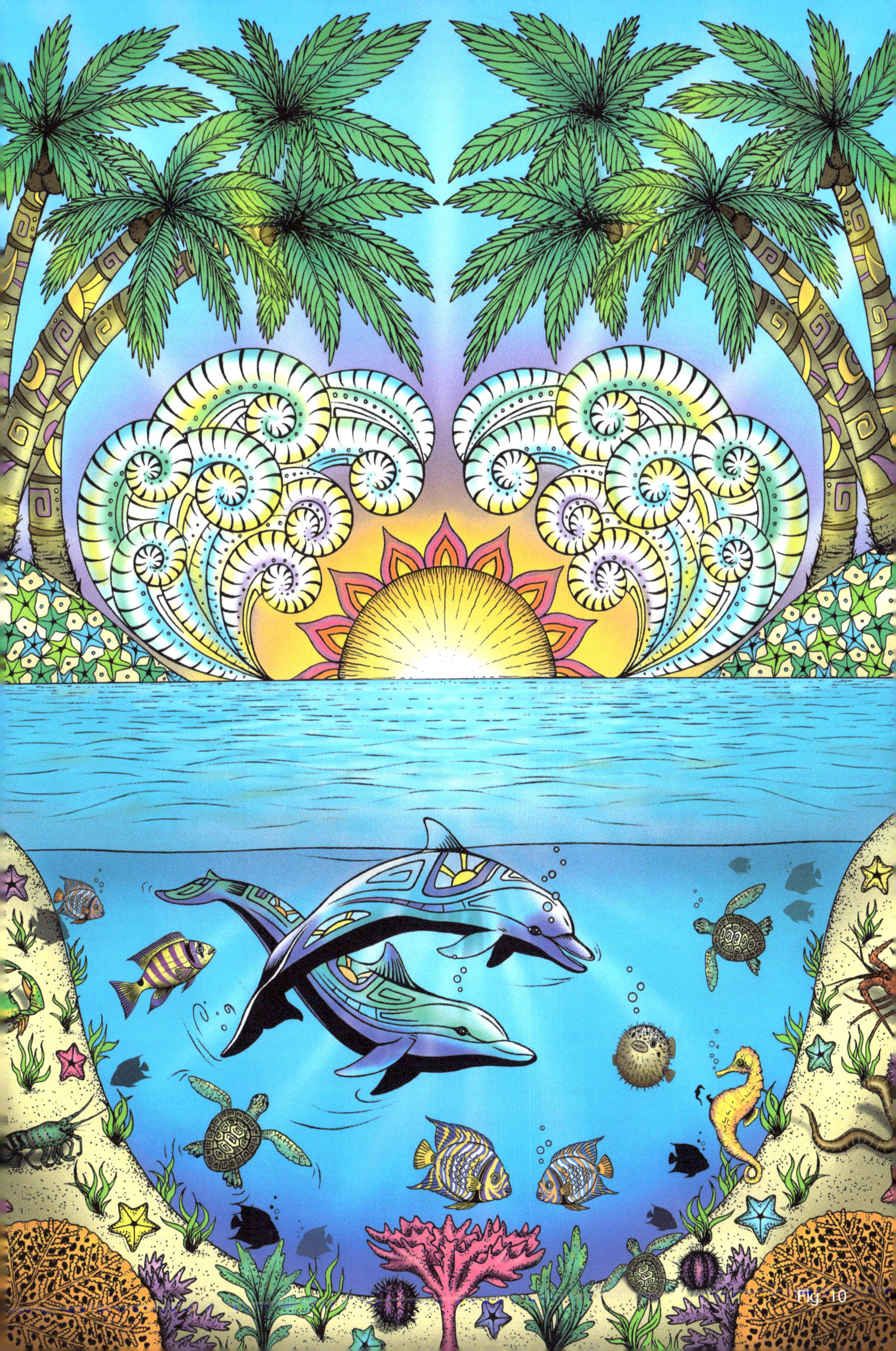

Fig. 10

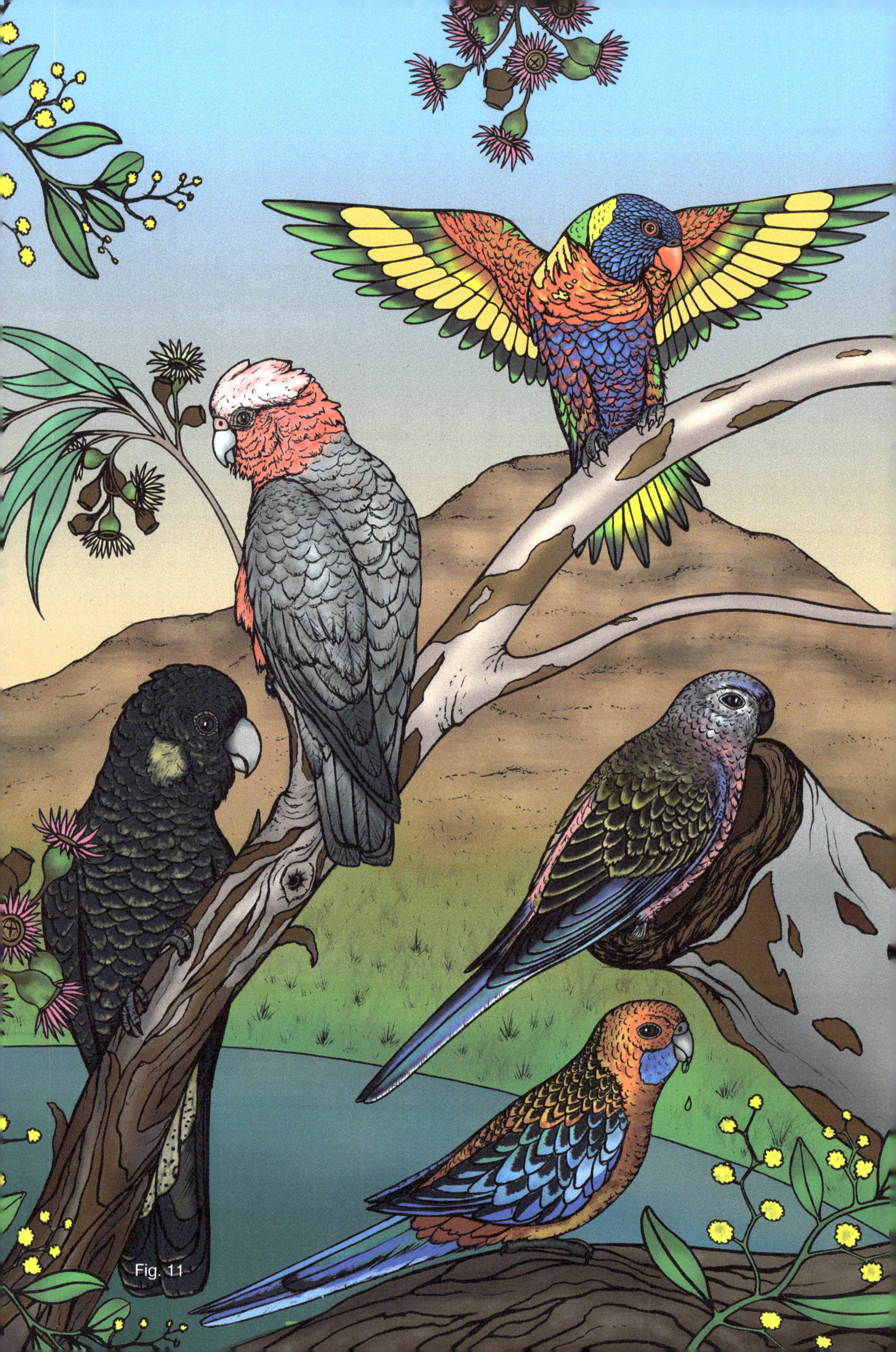

Fig. 11

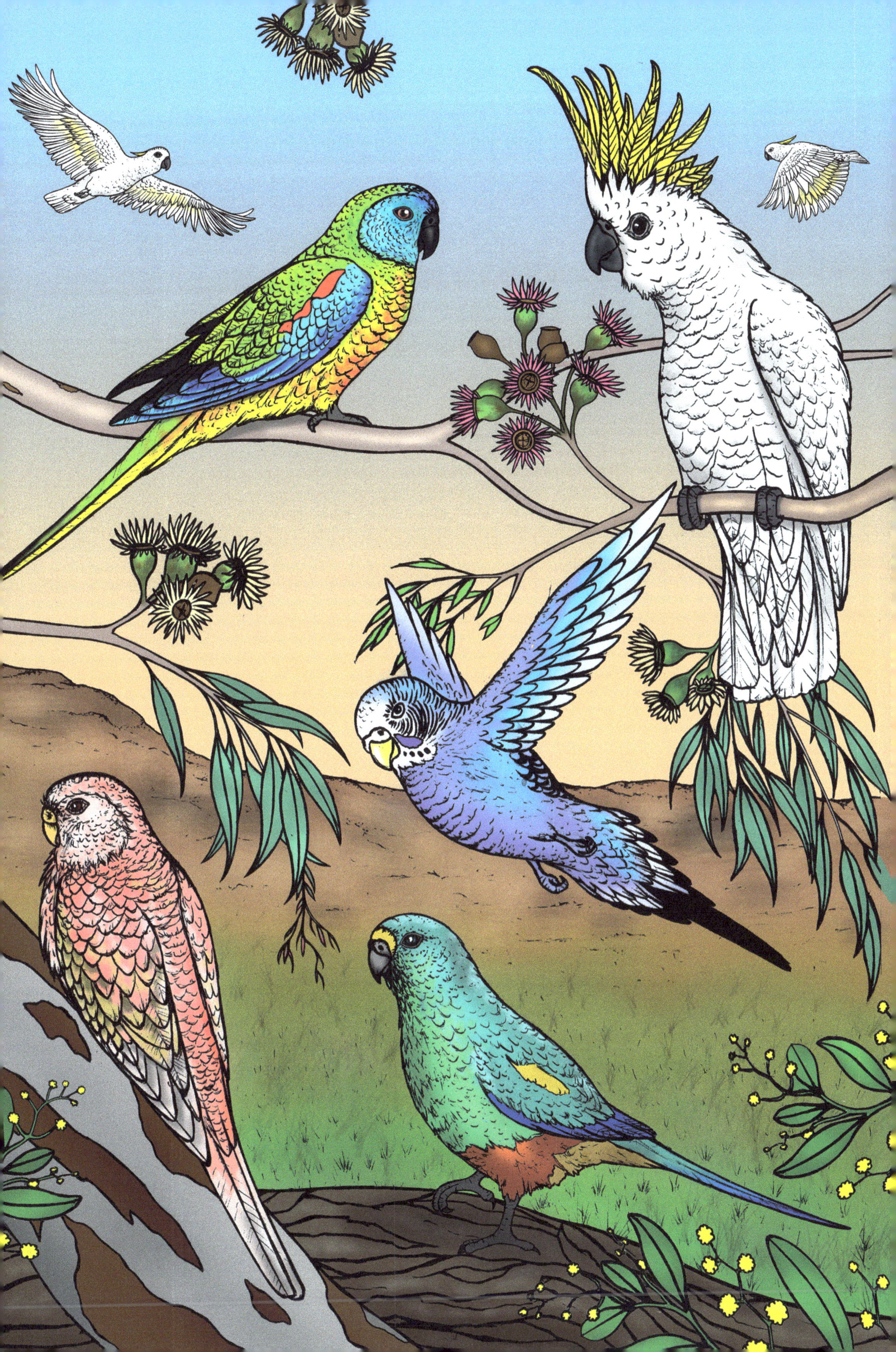

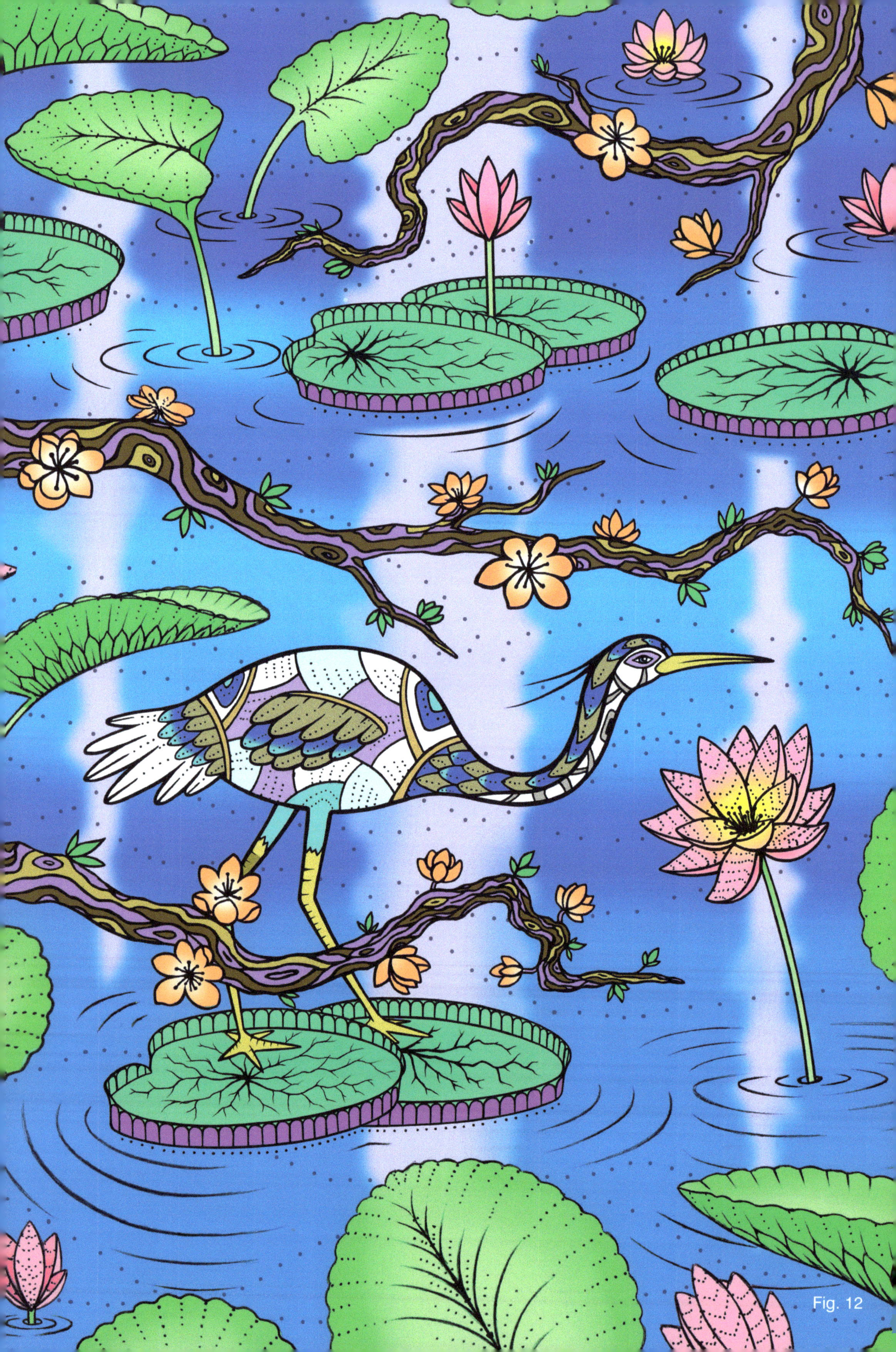

Fig. 12

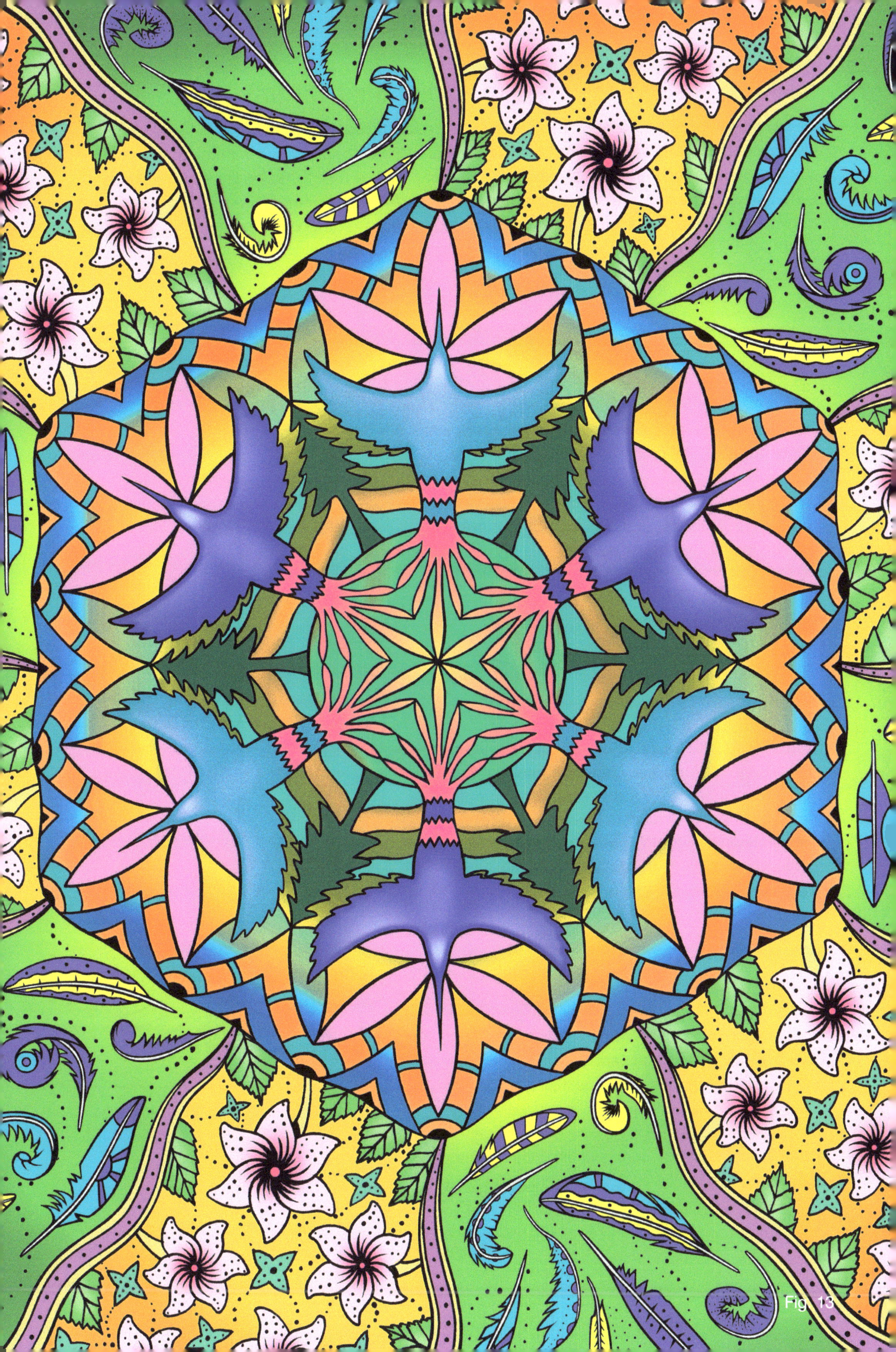

Fig. 13

Masterclass 4: Drawing and Inking Bird Totems

This exercise is focused on achieving both balanced symmetry and visually appeasing graphic stylisation in line with tribal glyphs or tattoo-style art. Remember to take your time at the sketching stage as it often requires multiple attempts with pencil and eraser to define lines with a sense of symmetry and balance. Use the internet for references or actual photos of animals from different angles to familiarise yourself with the base geometry and overall body symmetry of your subject. Then once you have chosen your profile, jump right in and get sketching.

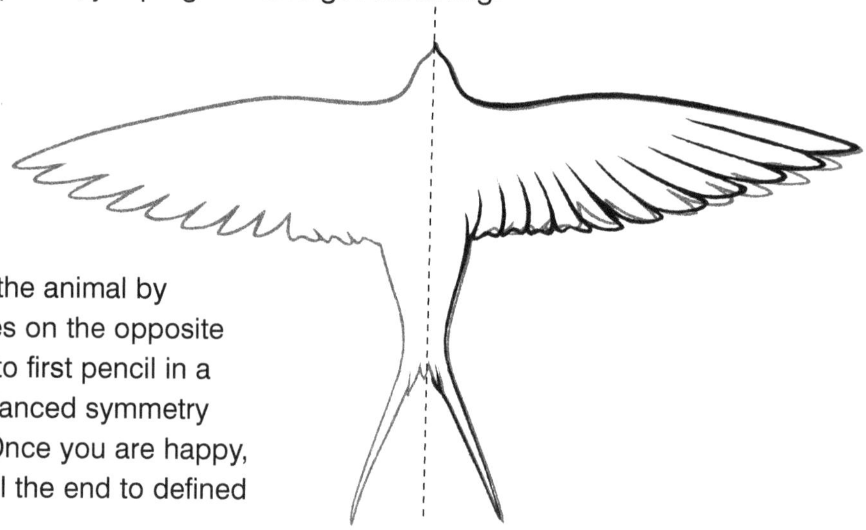

Step 1: Draw the outline image of the animal by simply copying one of the examples on the opposite page. If it is an aerial view it helps to first pencil in a centre line and practice getting balanced symmetry from right to left sides of the line. Once you are happy, you can ink this in pen, or wait until the end to defined the outline of the design.

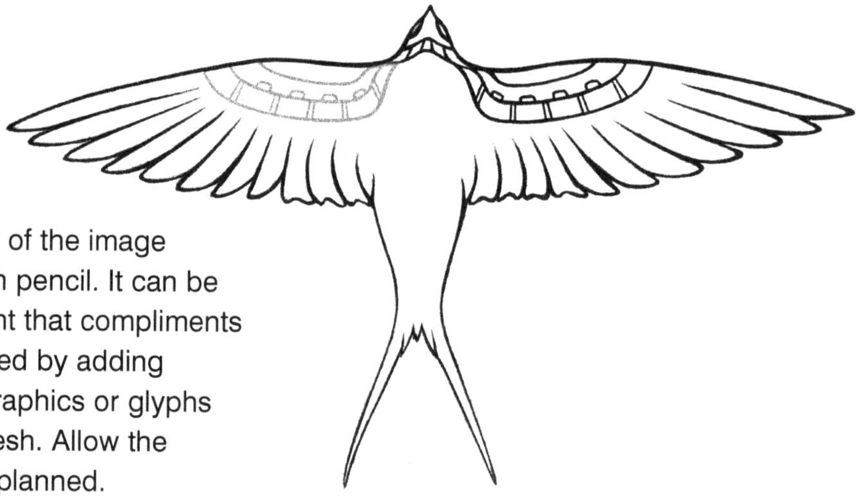

Step 2: Start with the head or belly of the image and detail in a graphic element with pencil. It can be elongated, circular, or a line element that compliments the animal or overall design. Proceed by adding complimentary design elements, graphics or glyphs that keep the design vibrant and fresh. Allow the process to be organic and not too planned.

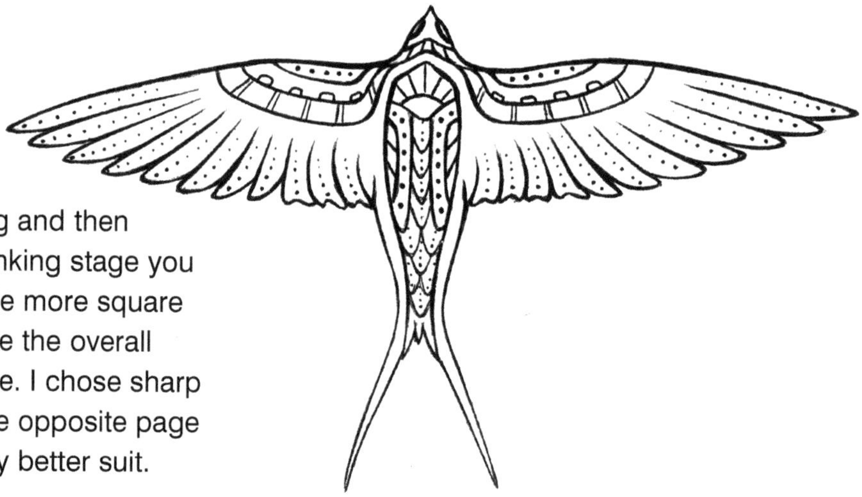

Step 3: Finish the design pencilling and then proceed to detailed inking. In the inking stage you can chose to make your lines a little more square or circular in design, which is where the overall character of the image comes to life. I chose sharp darty lines here for the swift. On the opposite page more segmented or wavy lines may better suit.

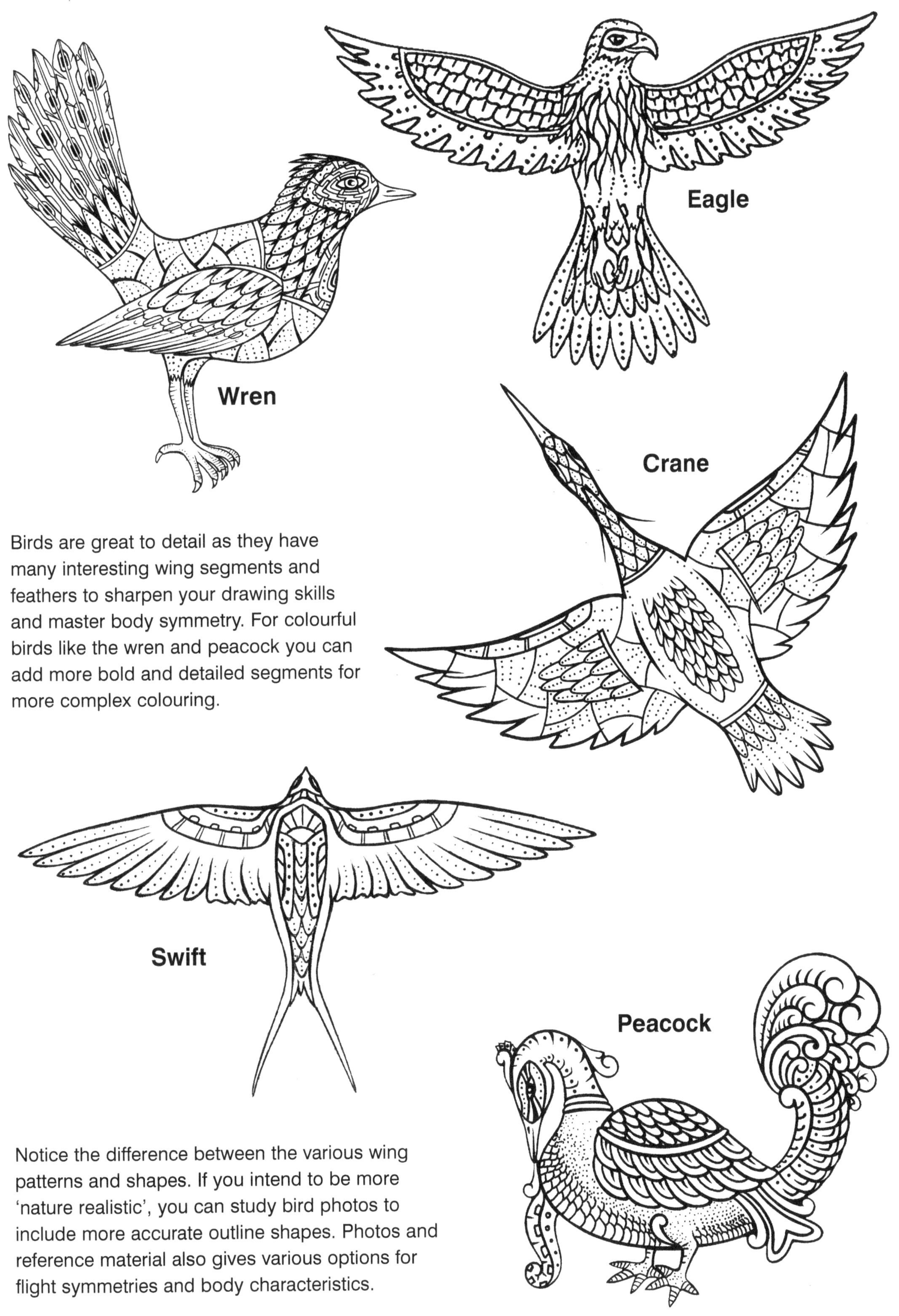

Birds are great to detail as they have many interesting wing segments and feathers to sharpen your drawing skills and master body symmetry. For colourful birds like the wren and peacock you can add more bold and detailed segments for more complex colouring.

Notice the difference between the various wing patterns and shapes. If you intend to be more 'nature realistic', you can study bird photos to include more accurate outline shapes. Photos and reference material also gives various options for flight symmetries and body characteristics.

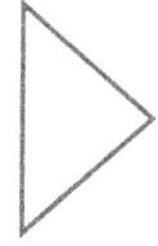

Hummingbirds are totems for transformation and the change from one state of creation to another. Hummingbird energies can be helpful for moving through creative blocks and personal emotional hurdles. Colours for more direct transformation could be red, orange, yellow. Alternatively try violets and pinks, with pastel rainbow colours or complementary opposites. This is also a great example of how to detail mandalas in the associated masterclasses and drawing designs on the following pages to create outer sections and more diverse and dynamic colouring panels.

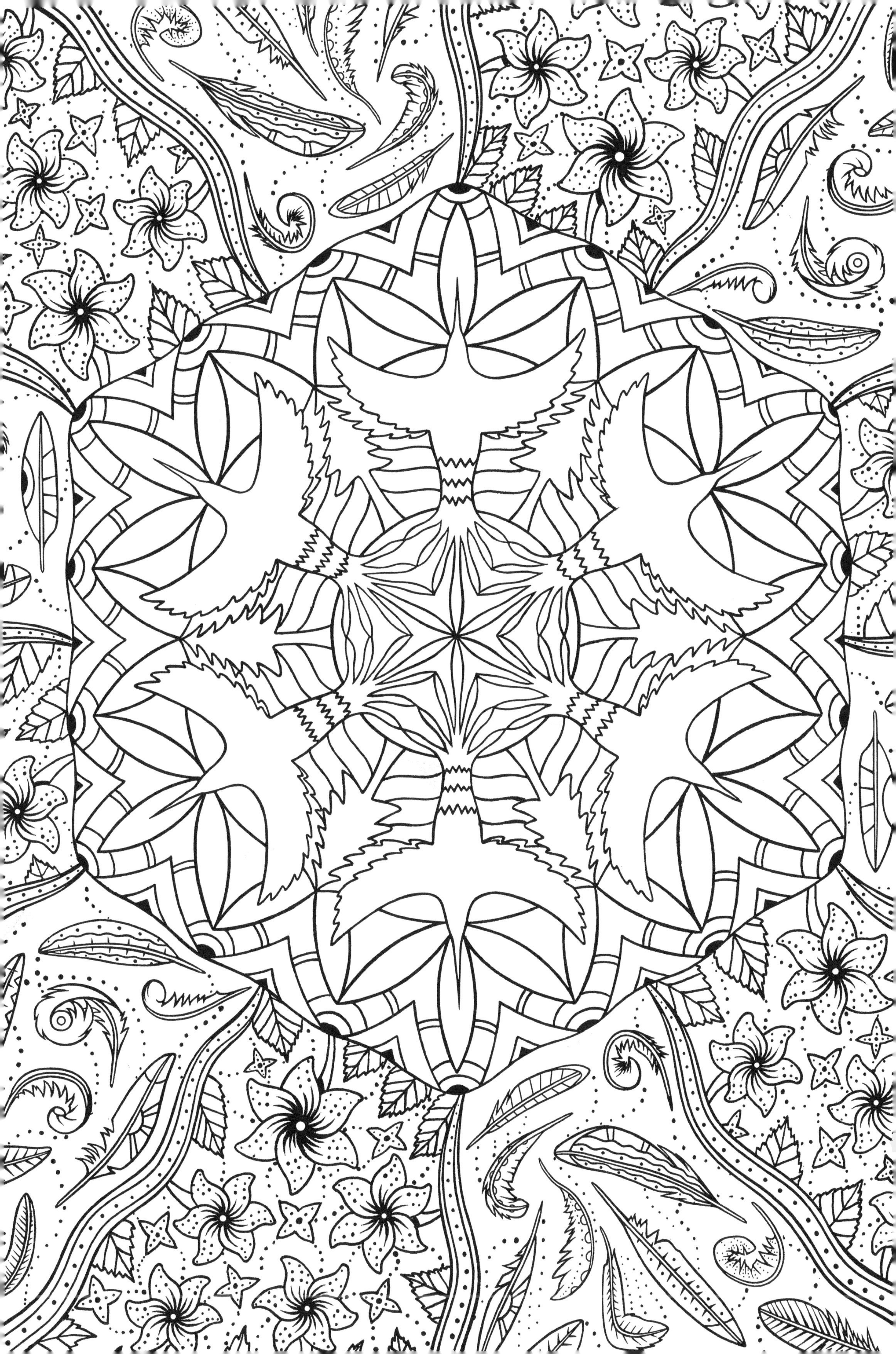

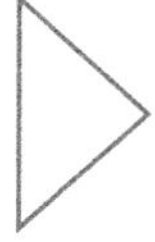

Wolves symbolise loyalty, group spirit and the principle of interrelationship. The image relates to the receptivity of Nature's life cycles and the culmination of these as we see in the full Moon. The wolf totem symbolises faithfulness and furthering a closeness to the very spirit of nature. Representing here mainly earth and water energies, colouring for the image can be predominantly blue, aqua and green tones. Mid earthy browns can add complimentary effects. Likewise, tan or sandy cream tones may work well, contrasting mid aquas or deep teal tones. The night sky works well with deep blue and indigo hues. The water can be turquoise of soft aqua blue and white to capture the effect of moonlight. These are just a few examples of colour combinations, yet in the spirit of the wolf, feel free to 'trust' your own colour interpretation for the image.

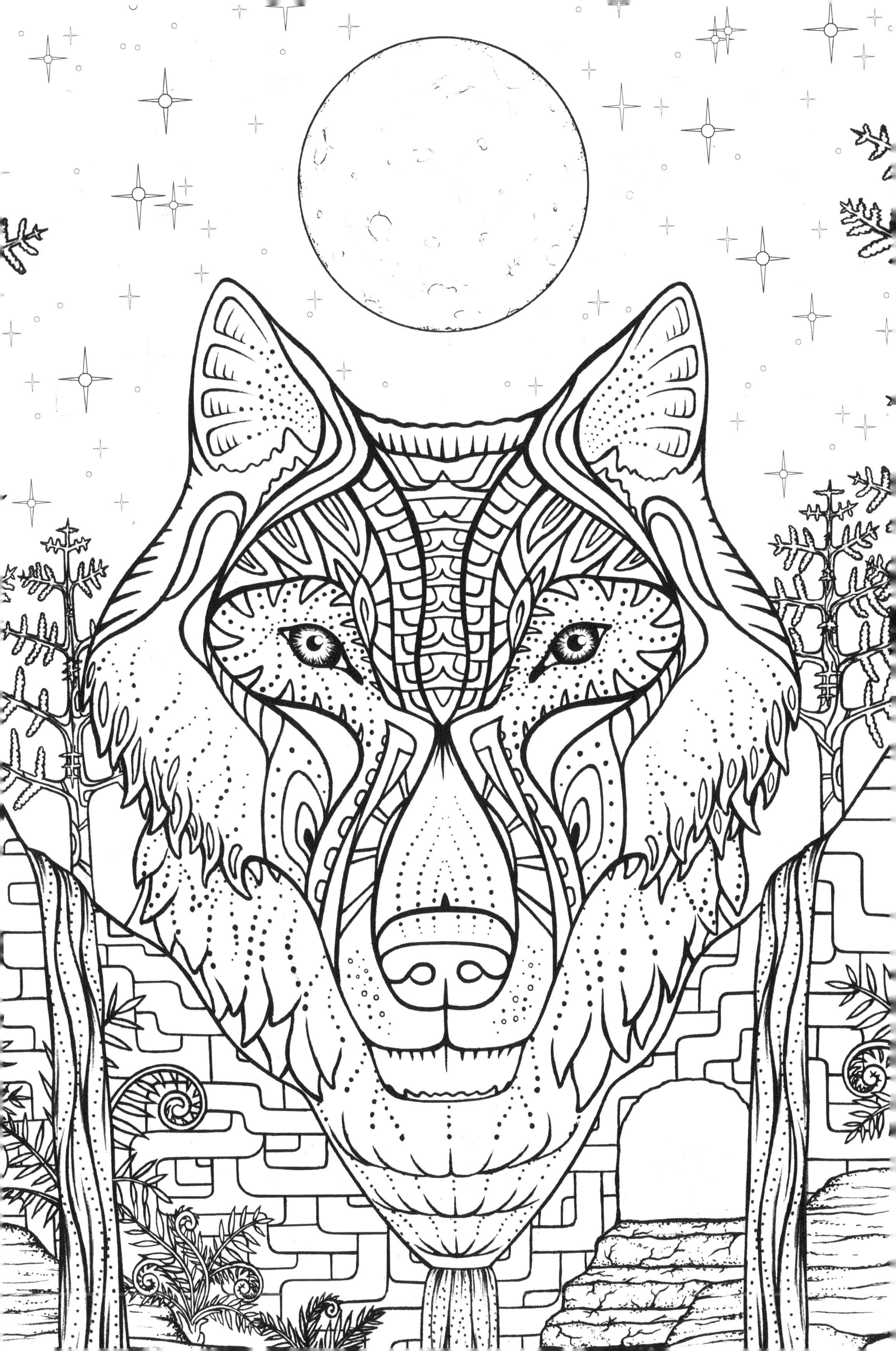

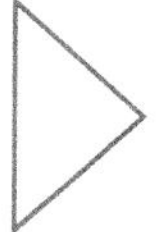

This stylised graphic design is in the tattoo style and has been coloured relative to the totems and animal's natural settings. Stylised water elements for the Manta ray at bottom relates to the indigo, blue and aqua hues. The best way to colour this panel and avoid clashing colours was to colour a section or element of the design with the next adjacent element or section in mind. So the indigo, blue and aqua colours for the bottom half of the image were alternated and colour was built up to create a balancing and pleasing effect. Likewise with the top section, where colours for the earth and sun were chosen. For a colour example see Fig. 9 at the front colour section of the book.

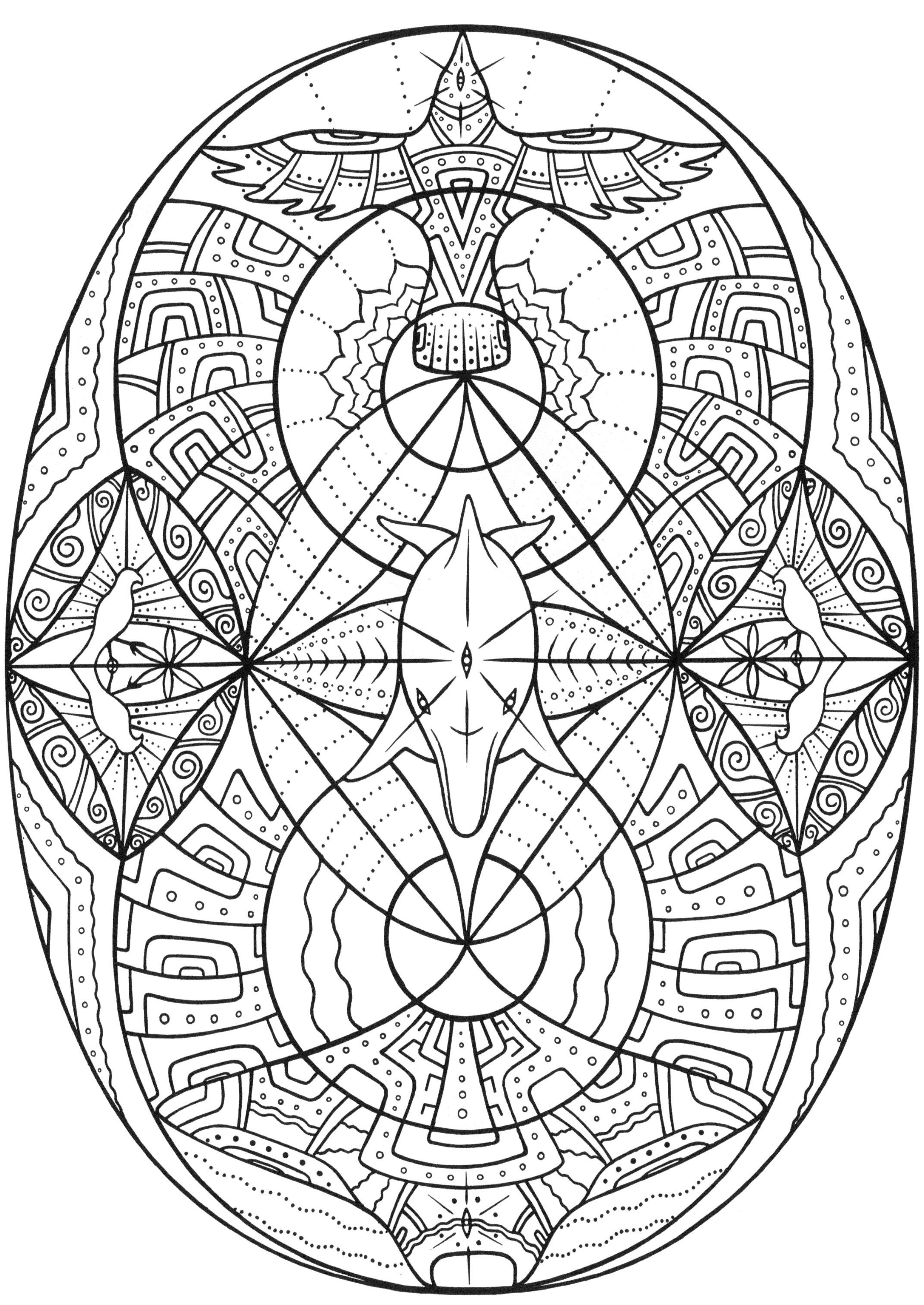

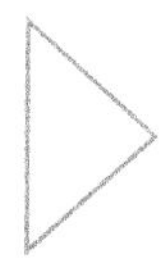

Parrots have an intricate connection to passion and love in many traditions and legends. They represent the will of desire and zest for life. The parrots here are highly stylised to show how detailed you can go with what would otherwise be a line drawing or more simplistic graphic design. Fell free to experiment with nature-identical colours from references, or include complementary opposites that you feel mat be right for the image. Some element may be sun rays, a rainbow maybe, clouds, trees and feathers. Subtle shading would also be effective in this image.

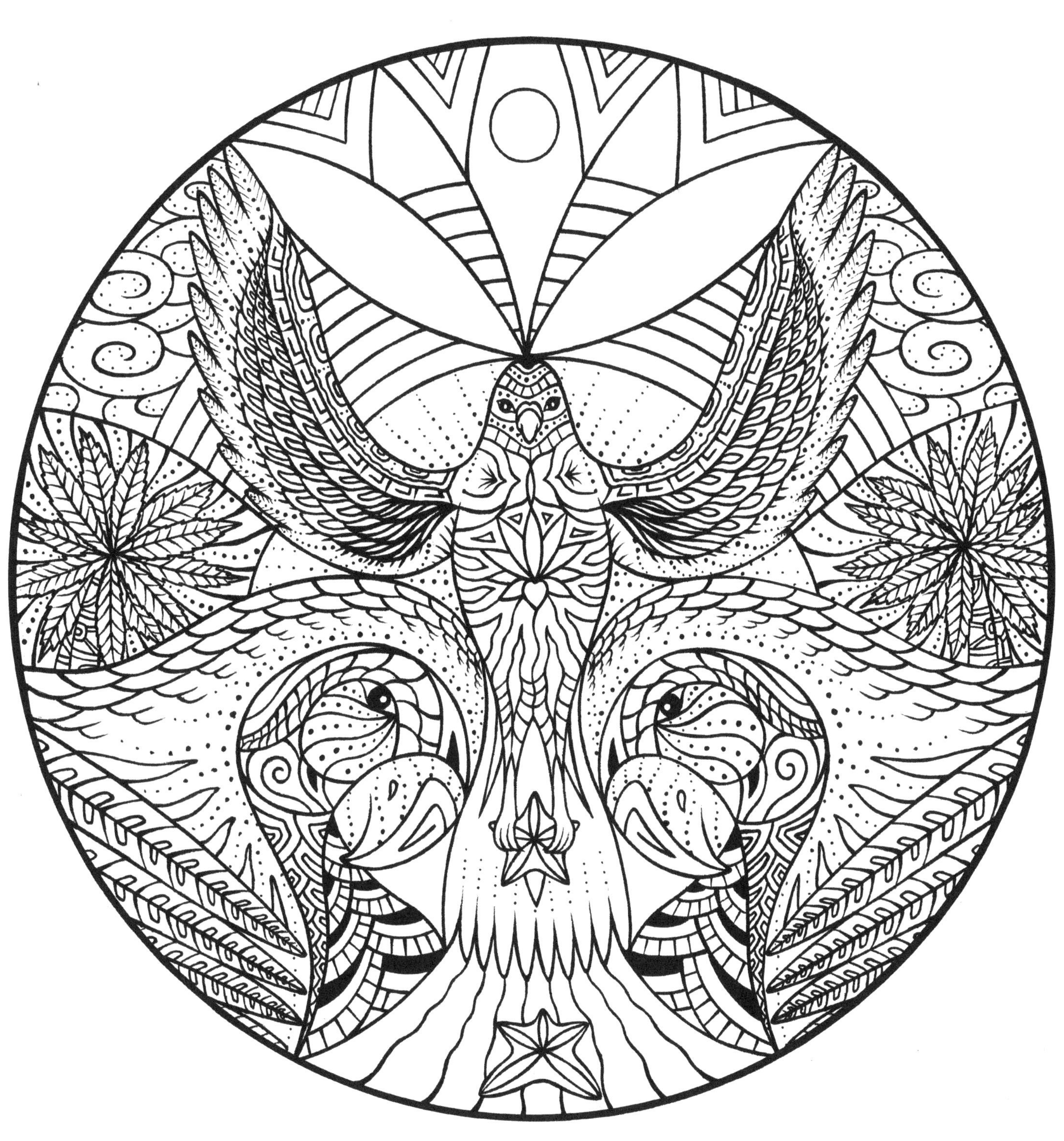

This nature mandala conveys the emerging energies of nature. The morning sun represents the light and inspiration of a new day, as does the central butterfly, indicating new beginnings, harmony and the spirit of freedom. The unicorn is a mythical creature aligned with the principles of intuition and vision. It represents here grace, harmony and the power of insight. In this image the snake signifies latent potential energy representing the hidden or unknown. So the overall syntax of the image is aligned with what would awaken personal power wisdom for new potential and new beginnings in your life. Golden hues and compeimentary opposites of violet may be a good colour choice, or maybe balance some bold powerful colours with aquas or greens.

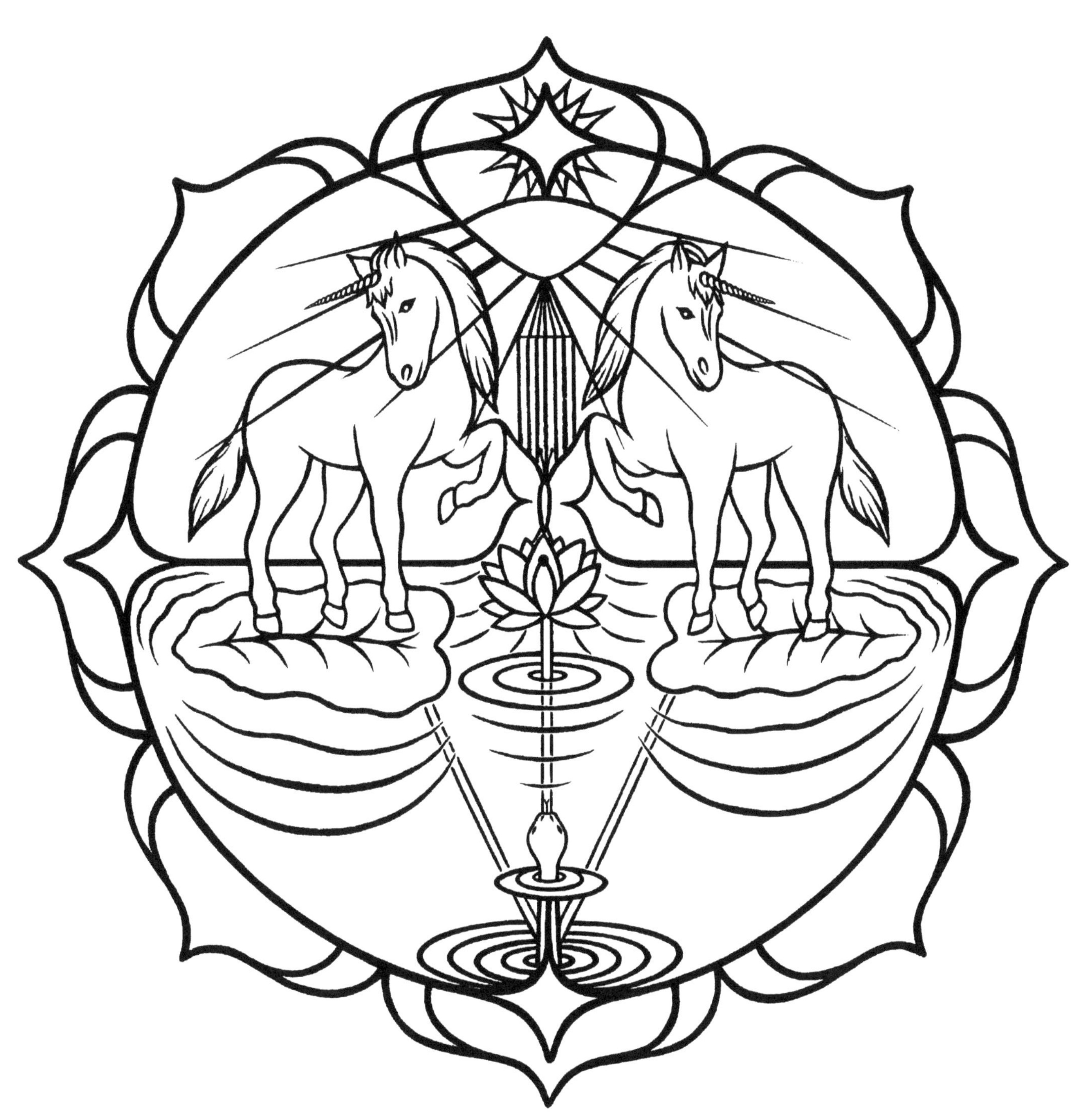

Masterclass 5: Graphic Detailing for Animals and Creatures

Study the graphic elements and stylised markings below. They give various examples of ways to further detail projects or colouring panel elements. Aim to allow a sense of freedom in your design stylings and it is often helpful to complement elements as you go and not plan ahead too much. Alternate square or segmented markings with dots or interlaced patterns detailed with dots, small circles or whatever comes to mind.

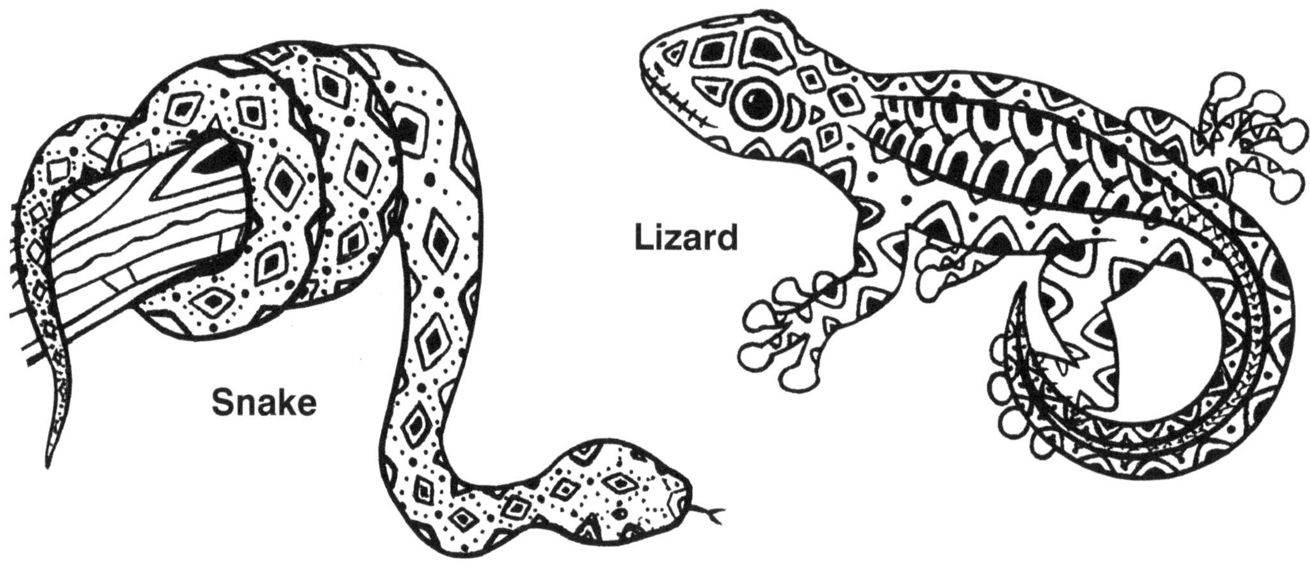

SNAKE: Snakes and lizards work well with banded markings and square or diamond shapes, which can mimic scale or skin patterns. Banded graphic segments work well also on their spiralling tails.

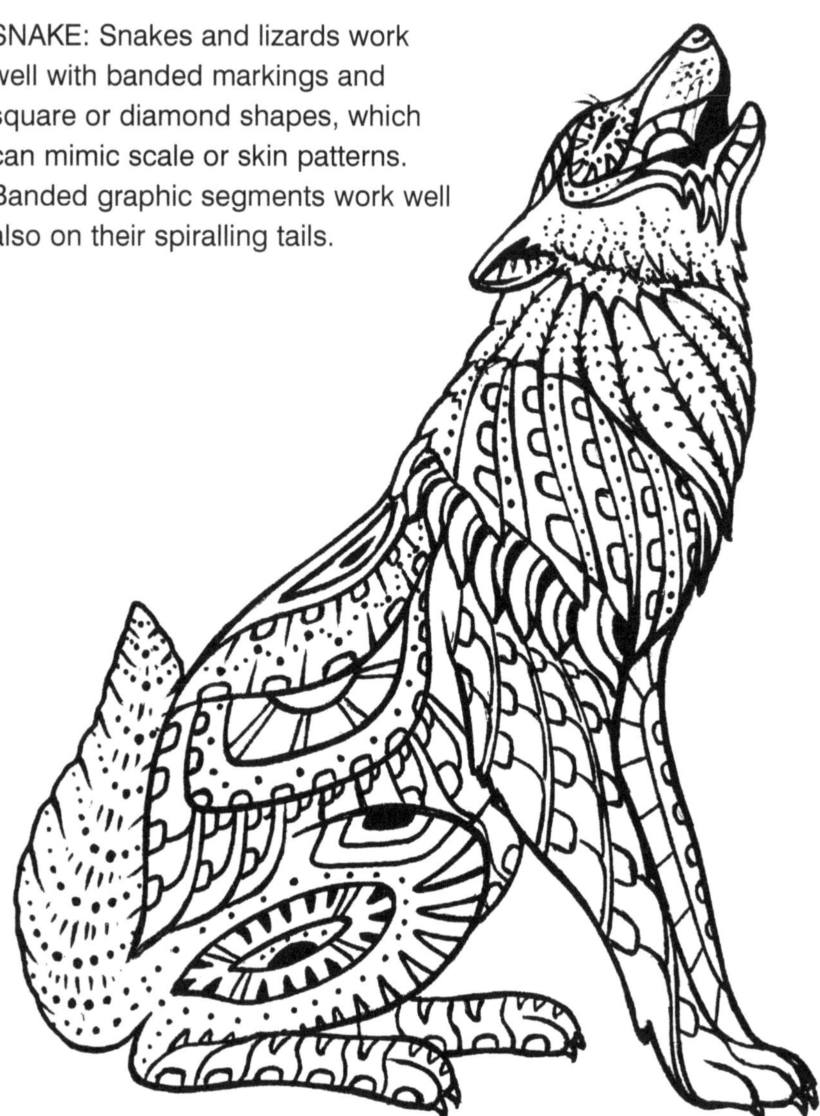

WOLF: This wolf here draws on Mesoamerican style glyphs and patterned markings. Line segments that mirror the wolf's characteristics like claws and teeth are added for emphasis and to complement otherwise more regular banded patterns.

Detailing Ocean and Sea Creatures

Sea creatures are fascinating subjects to detail and you can use more fluid shapes to mimic their surroundings. Watery environments give a certain movement to their forms like they are floating or gliding, being suspended by the body of the ocean. There are also many diverse species to keep our creative juices flowing, as the sea symbolises the birth of form and very origins of life.

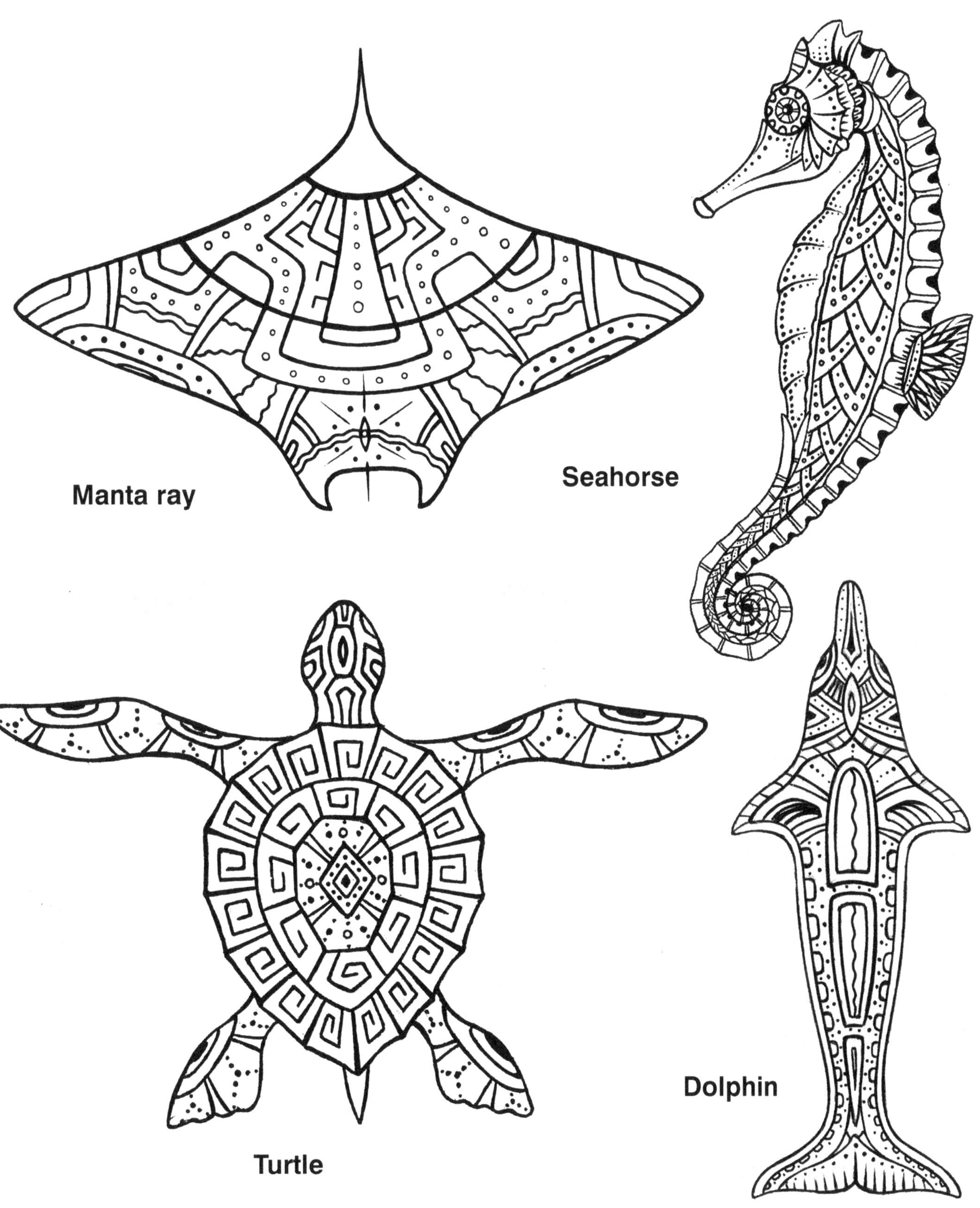

EXERCISE: Detailing The Manta Ray from the Ocean's Deep

Detail the opposite half of the manta ray in either duplicate markings, or try some unique styling of your own. Wavy lines and segments can be alternated with more square or defined lines. The small circles were added in the example below to mimic bubbles from the ocean world.

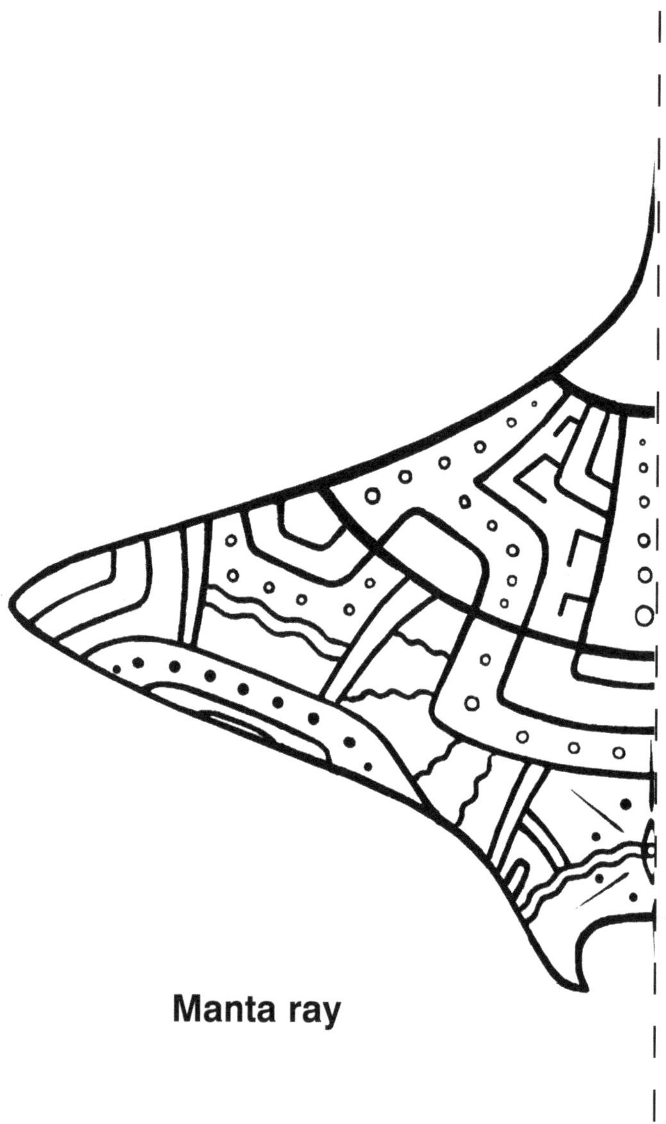

Manta ray

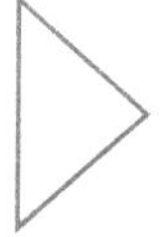

The wolf totem has already been covered on page 26 in association with loyalty, kinship and inter-connectedness. A good totem to work with to ground ourself, or find our sense of home and where our loyalties lie. Colour the example here in earthy colours maybe, or use it as an exercise to trace the outline shape and detail some of your own graphic elements or designs.

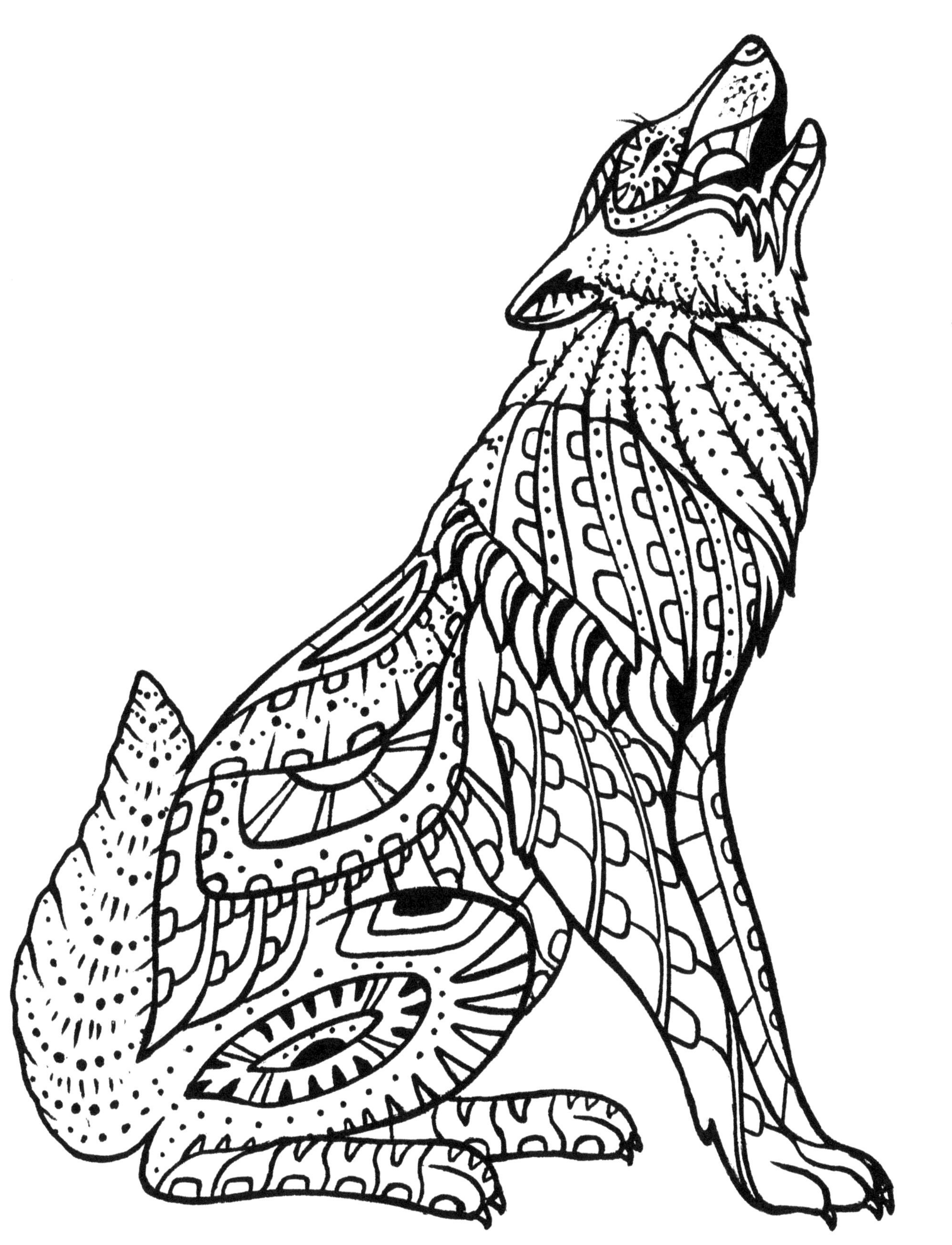

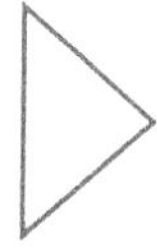

What colouring book would be complete without some baby wolf cubs to colour? Their eyes here echo a mix of vulnerability, kinship and trust. As stated earlier, the wolf totem is associated with loyalty and the principle of interrelationship. It is a good totem to work with to foster a closeness to the very spirit of nature and Mother Earth. We'd all do well to reclaim a bit of child-like innocence towards Mother Earth. Here we have innocence and vitality on account of the youthful and playful qualities of the juvenile cubs. Soft and gentle pastel colours can be well suited, or try colours for youthfulness and vitality, like variegated green, tan and aqua hues.

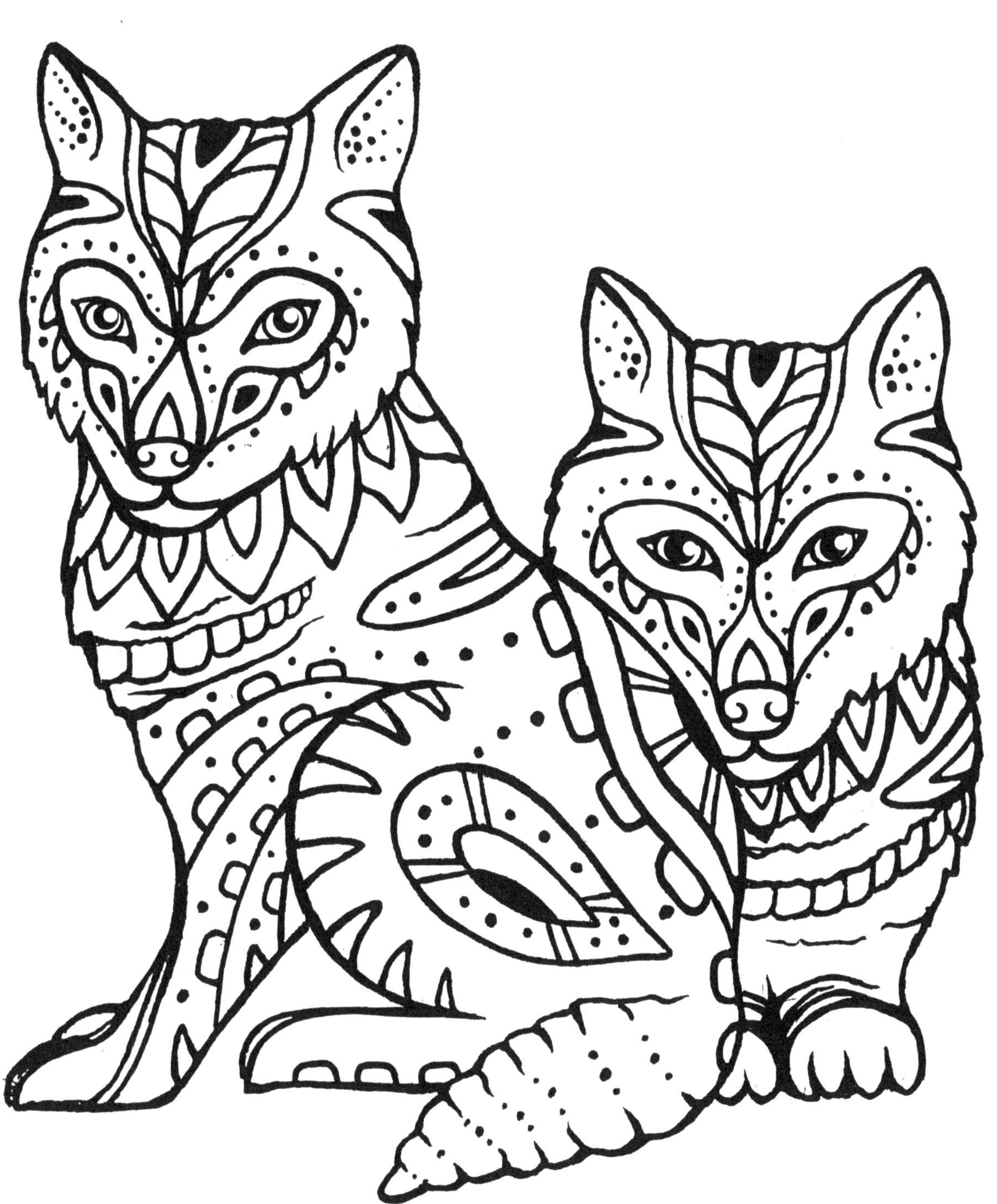

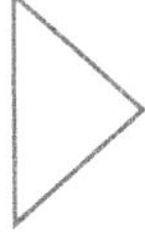

A more detailed and stylised ocean panel with diverse sea creatures to colour freely is included on the following page. This could be cut out and copied for a larger panel. Elements from the previous two exercises can be helpful to re-invent yourself or work outside of the logical thought process of the concrete mind. Ocean scenes are vibrantly alive with possibilities and we can aim to include a balance or nature-identical and stylised imagery for a more creative and insightful colouring journey. Alternatively, just colour freely as a form or relaxation or to calm and soothe the mind. Ocean scenes are great for this, as they often involve a predominance of blue tones in deep blue, indigo and aqua. Then complimentary opposite colours like yellow and orange can be added for fish and corals. There is a colour version of this in the front colouring section of the book and a full analysis of how the colours were chosen for this rendering.

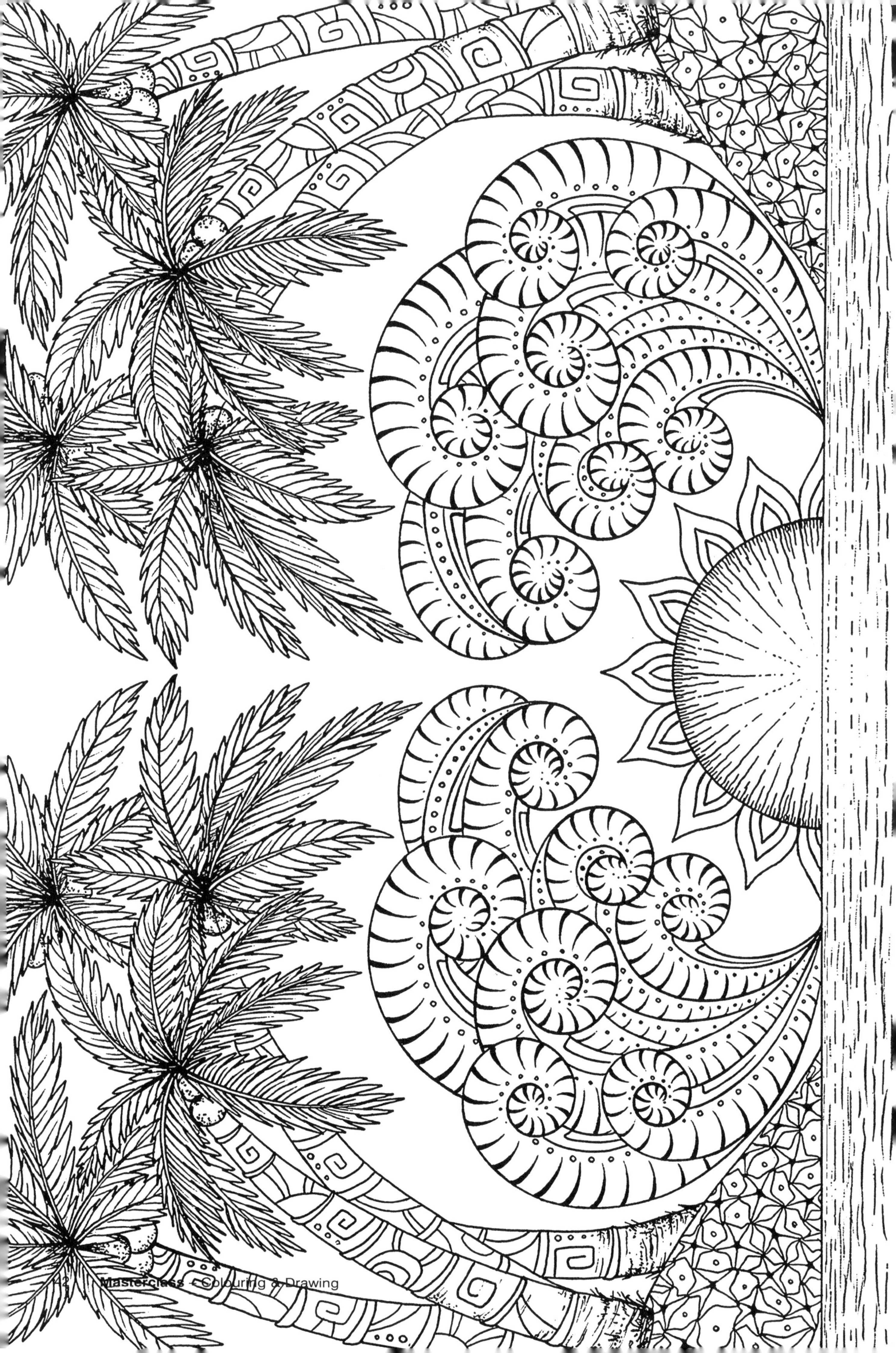

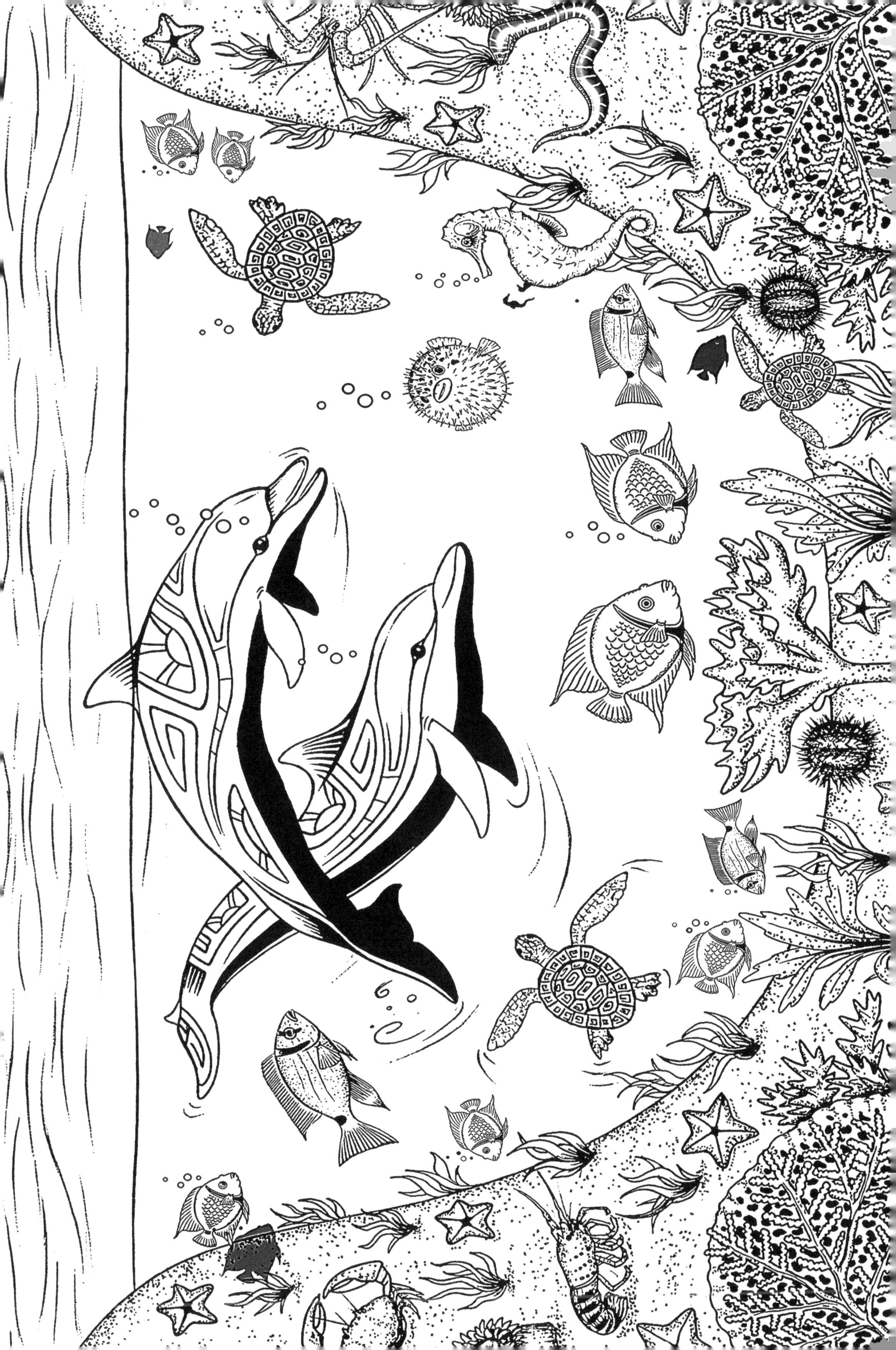

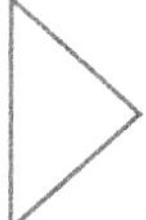

This colouring panel uses more stylised animals and graphics from the masterclasses 4 and 5. Peacocks relate to the majesty and glory of creation and are held sacred amongst many Eastern cultures and traditions. The Peacock has a special association with the forest. Likewise, the reptiles here are from forest or woodland areas and the depiction has a sub-tropical kind of feel. It has been constructed as a two-page panel so that more detail in colouring can be achieved. The peacock naturally relates well to blue and green hues, with the lizard and snakes possibly any colour that takes your fancy or that compliments the image. The snake totem is diverse in its meaning and application, this application is a more gentle or playful tree snake. The lizard is here an inquisitive forest gecko, related to creativity, dreaming or musing with a sense of innocence and wonder.

Peacocks are masters of attentiveness and denote a keen watchfulness over foundational matters and the process of creation. In their depth of focus there is a mastery of time associated with this totem, that relates to a special condensed energy of the present moment. This is where they gain their association with the majesty of creation and symbolise grace and favour. They further relate here to principles like fortitude, endurance and a certain pride in the power or glory of the creation process.

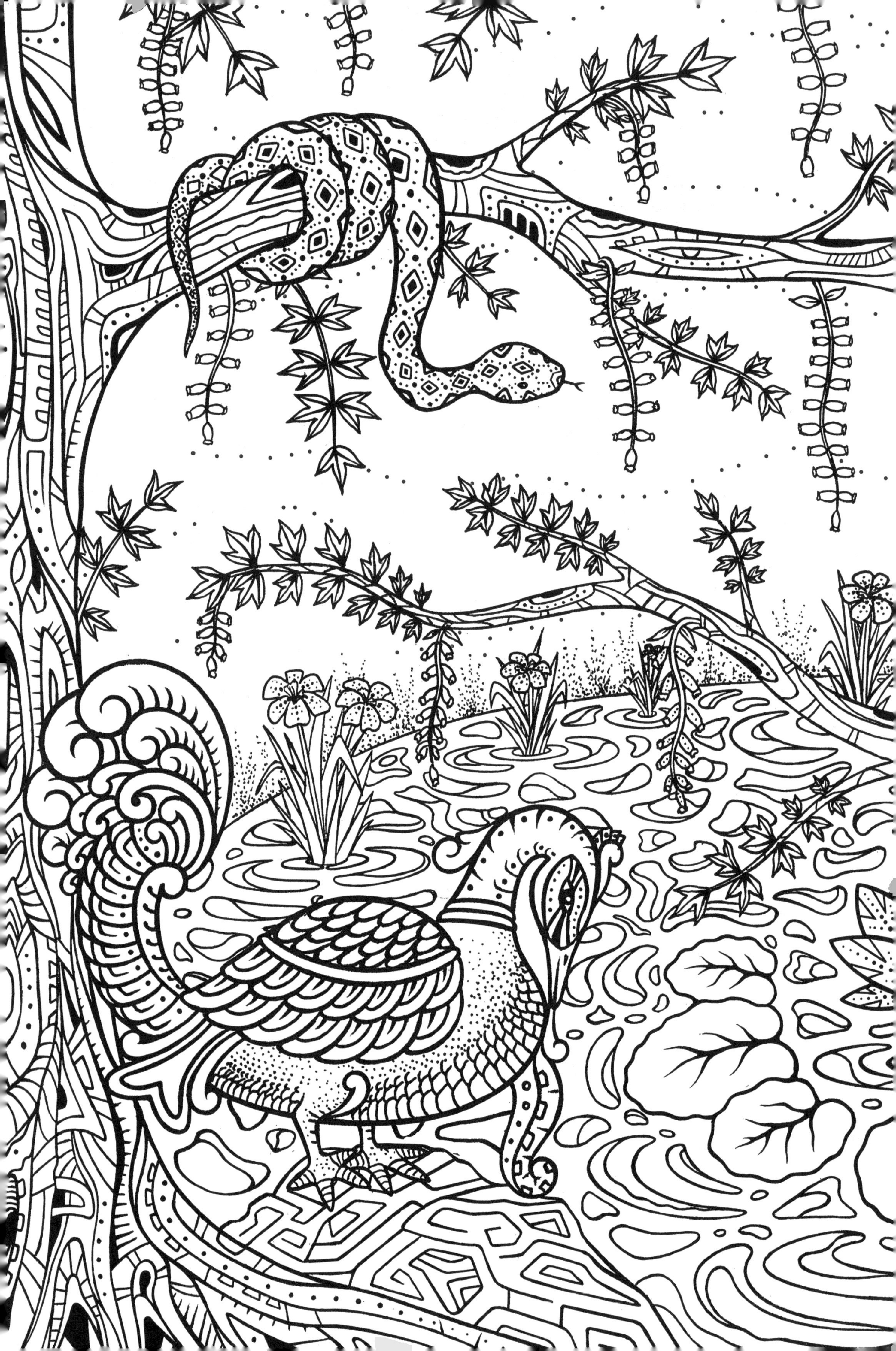

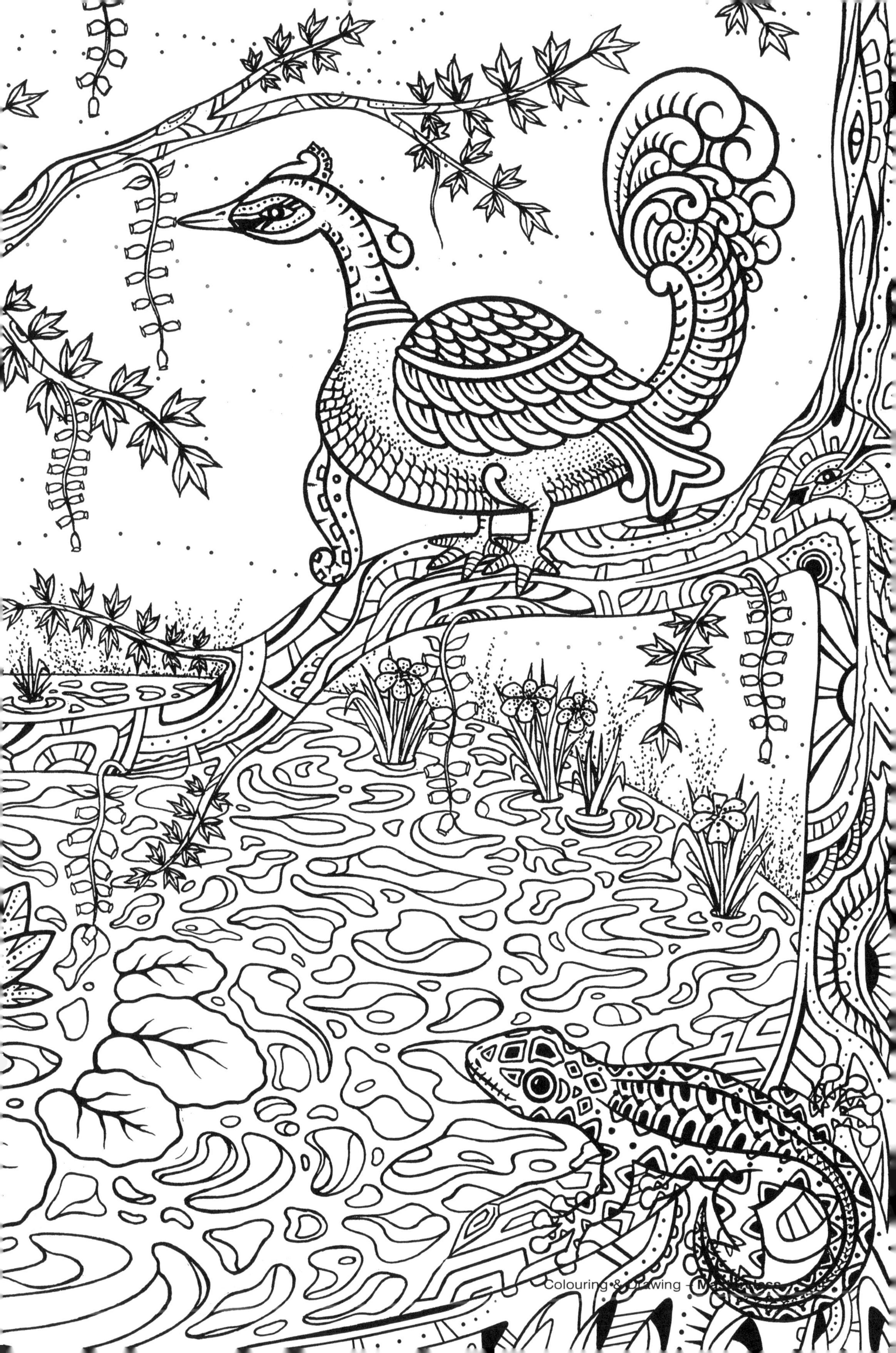

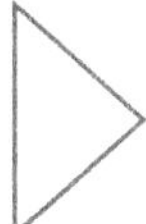

This panel is in honour of my late father, who brought much inspiration growing up with his large collection of birds, from parrots, finches, doves and quails. Parrots were his favourite and this panel has been created in a more nature-realistic and less stylised manner to appreciate the uniqueness and colouring potential with this area of Australian wildlife. Parrots have an intricate connection to passion and love in many traditions and folklore. They have been coloured here in their natural surroundings with nature-identical colour choices. You may choose to copy the coloured example from the front colouring section or go with your own colours, the choice is yours. The one thing with Australian parrots is that they are given to colour mutation, which is evident in the pink bourke parrot at bottom left of the right-hand page.

The male bourke is at middle left on the left hand page on the same log. Other birds in the image are the black cockatoo and pink galah at the very left of the image, with the rainbow lorikeet top right with fanned wings. The rosella drinking from the waterhole comes in variety of colours - this one is the Adelaide Rosella native to South Australia. Parrots in the right-hand panel are the turquoisine (top left) the Sulphur-crested cockatoo (top right), the budgerigar (in flight), which also comes in baby blue and aqua colours. The mulga parrot is a bright full colour male, which is important as the female parrots are often a different hue or can be softer or more muted in their colour palette. The flowers are just from native acacia and eucalyptus trees.

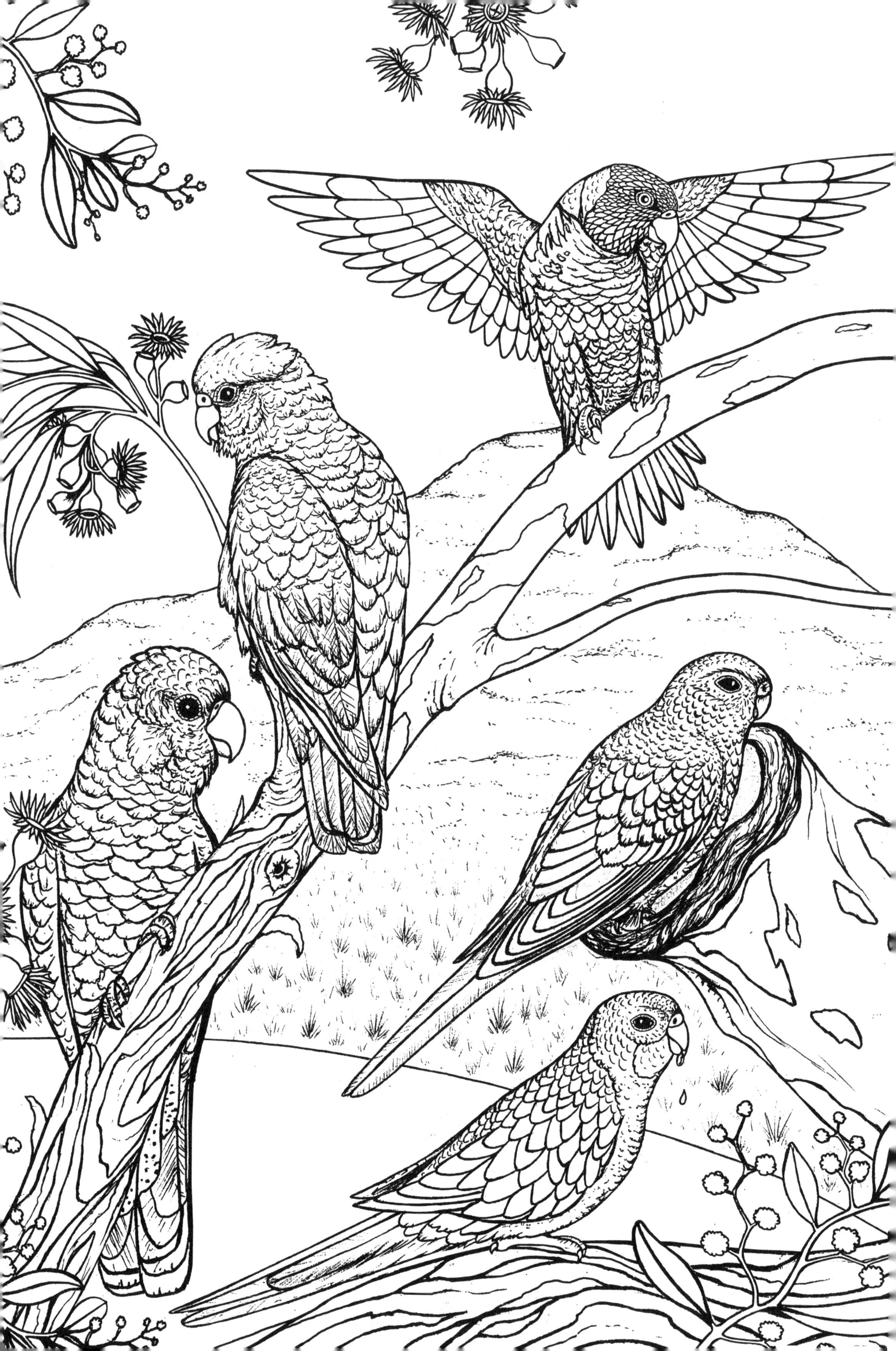

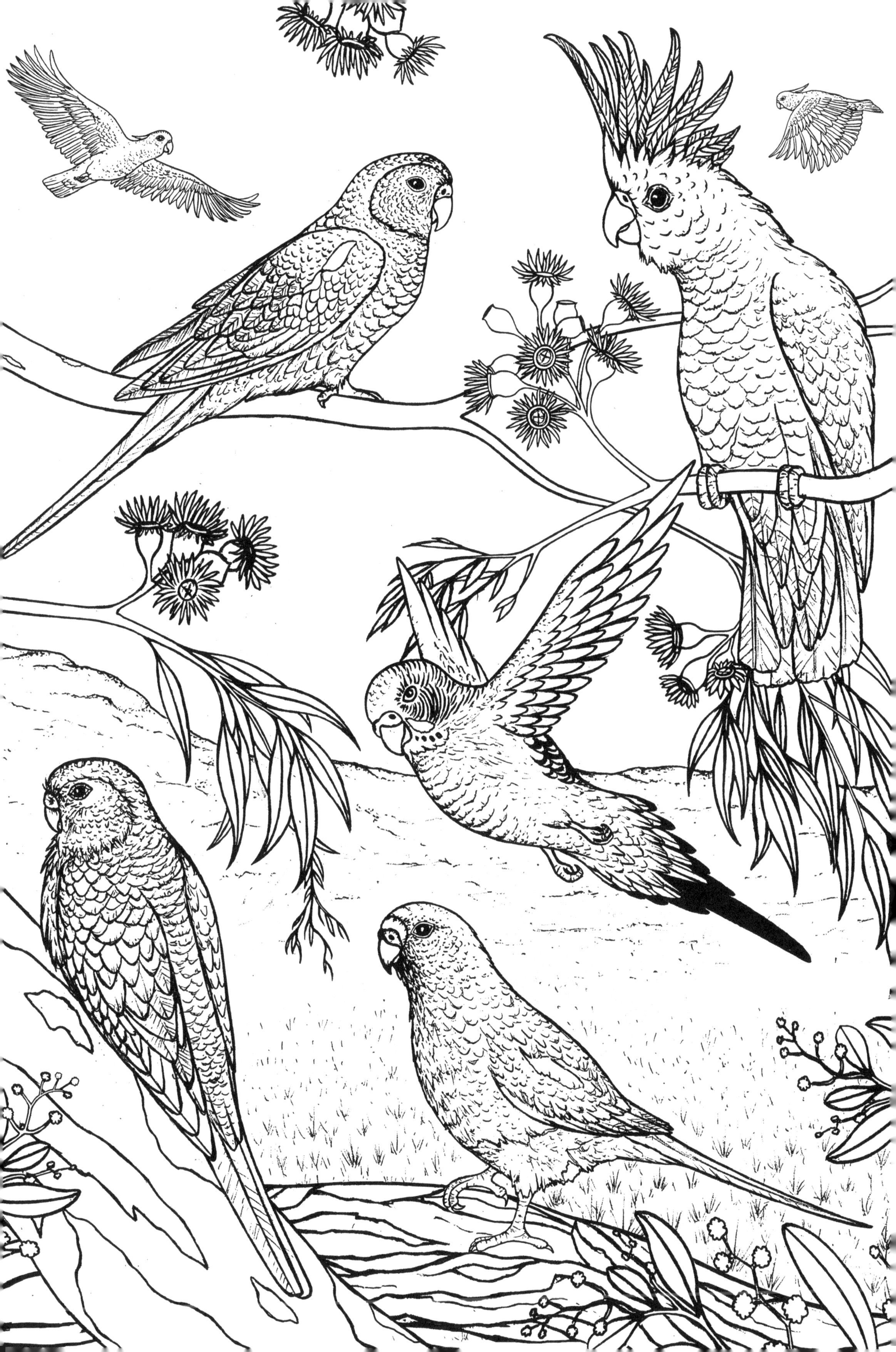

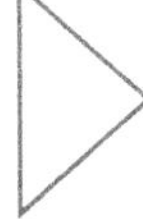

Cranes have for centuries been a totem associated with longevity, support and wisdom. They relate also to the ability to oversee or watch over others, an idea, or project, with the necessary intuition and discernment to see things through to fruition. They in this regard have an intricate connection to the rhythms of nature and cycles of time and can denote focus and self-reliance similar to the heron totem. This setting is a natural pond setting with lotuses and a watery environment lending itself well to blues, aquas and greens for the lotus leaves. The actual lotus flowers represent new life emerging and can be coloured in hues of your choice. Yellows and orange would give a complimentary effect if blues are chosen for water or the Crane, whereas violets and pinks could also work well for lotuses and lilies. The magnolias symbolise grace, harmony and enduring love, the type of love that has the tenacity to search or reach beyond the boundaries of time. They connect here to the longevity principle associated with the crane totem and are coloured orange to complement the rich blue hues. Pink magnolias could also be used, which represent the timeless nature and intimate connections to those we cherish or love. The Crane totem resonates to the Indigo (wisdom and insight) and blue/aqua (perseverance and support) hues. For a coloured example see Fig. 12 at the colour section of the book.

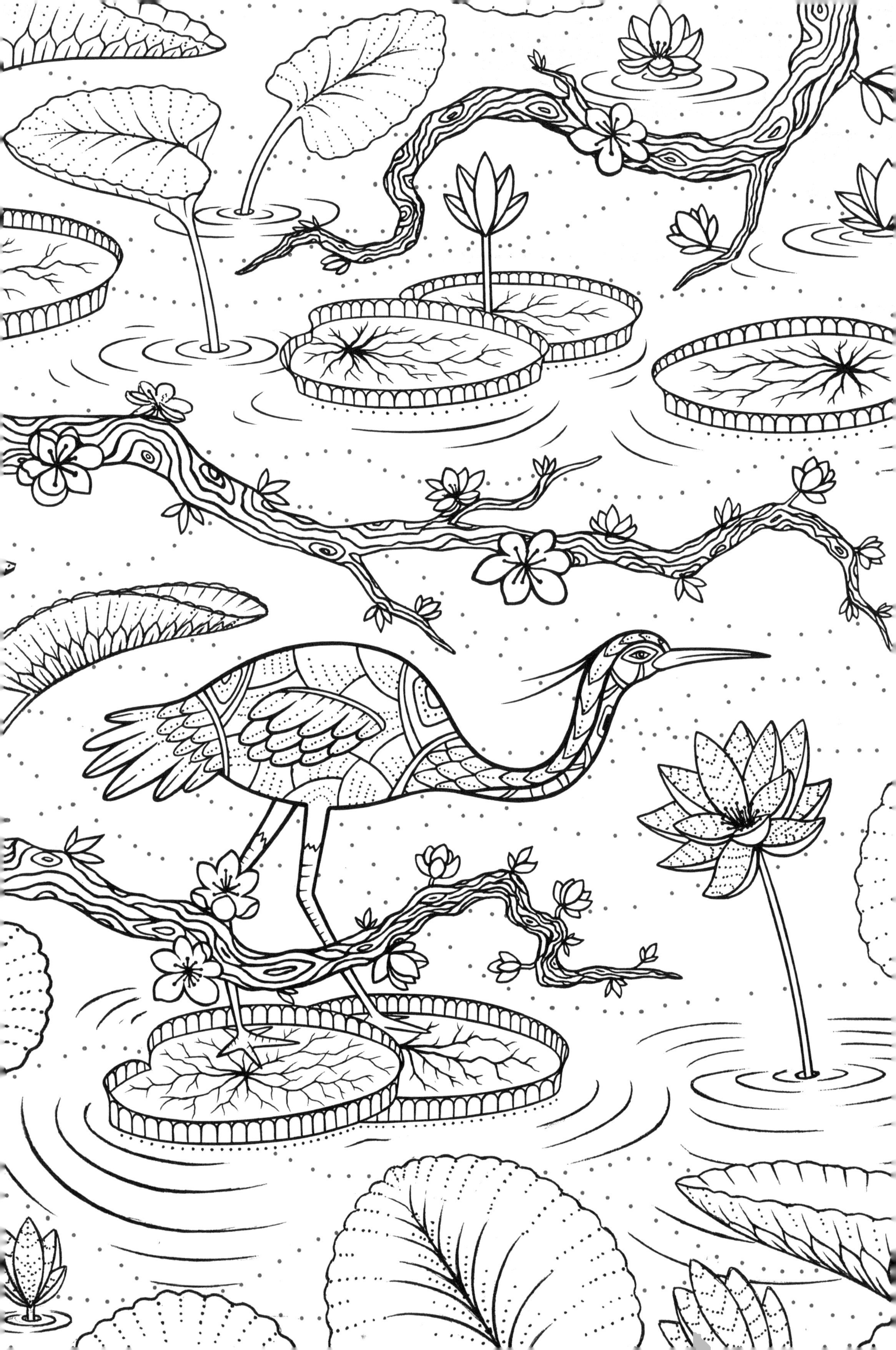

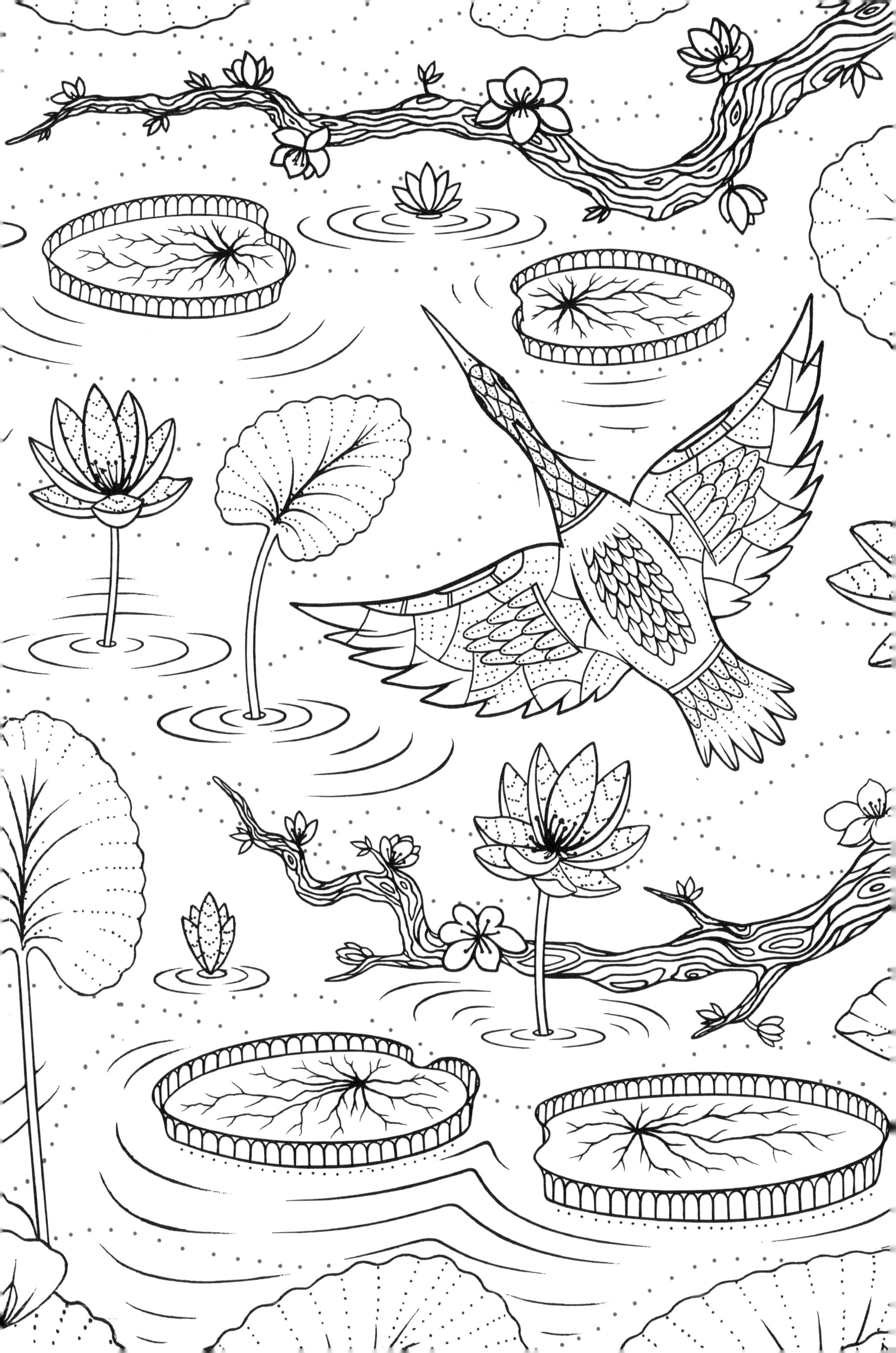

Masterclass 6: Drawing and Inking Stylised Tree Graphics

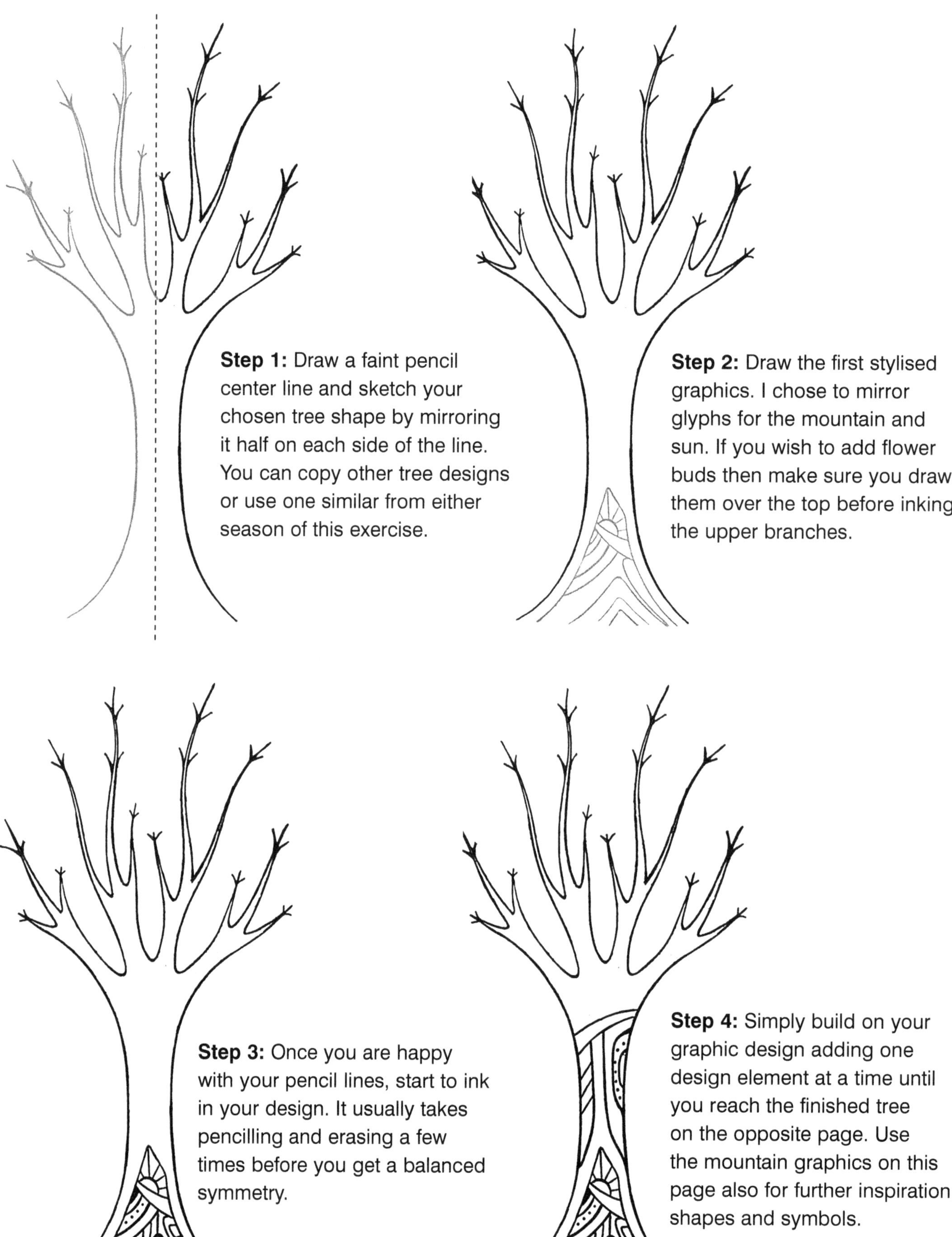

Step 1: Draw a faint pencil center line and sketch your chosen tree shape by mirroring it half on each side of the line. You can copy other tree designs or use one similar from either season of this exercise.

Step 2: Draw the first stylised graphics. I chose to mirror glyphs for the mountain and sun. If you wish to add flower buds then make sure you draw them over the top before inking the upper branches.

Step 3: Once you are happy with your pencil lines, start to ink in your design. It usually takes pencilling and erasing a few times before you get a balanced symmetry.

Step 4: Simply build on your graphic design adding one design element at a time until you reach the finished tree on the opposite page. Use the mountain graphics on this page also for further inspiration, shapes and symbols.

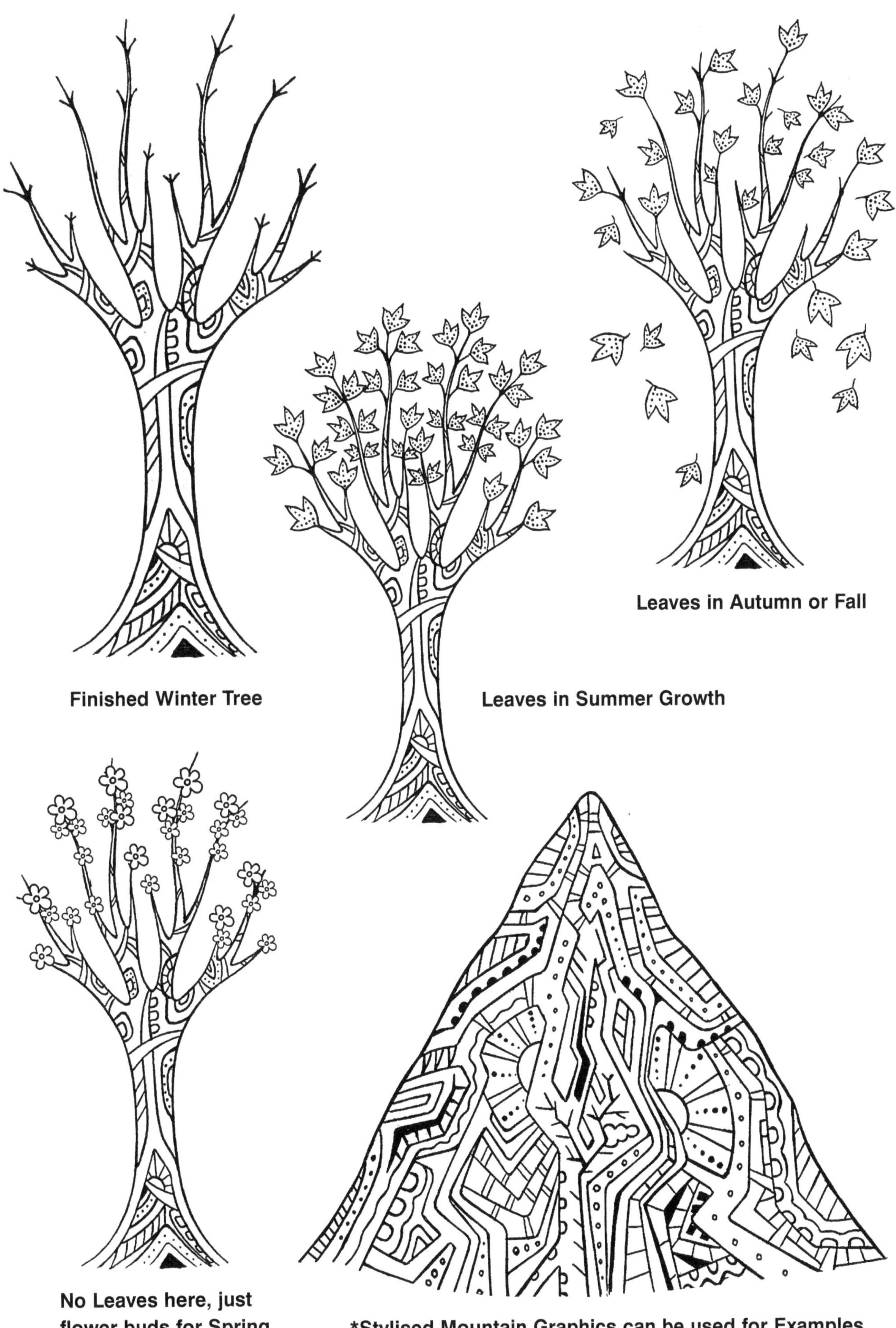

Finished Winter Tree

Leaves in Summer Growth

Leaves in Autumn or Fall

No Leaves here, just
flower buds for Spring

*Stylised Mountain Graphics can be used for Examples.

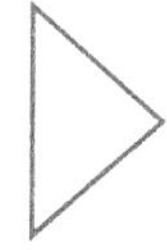

Seahorses are fascinating and enigmatic creatures that lend themselves to vivid and impactful artwork. The spiralling shapes of the seahorse relates to creative journeying. As a totem, the seahorse is good for working beyond fixed patterns and barriers and denotes abstract thinking and realms of creative possibility. Seahorses have a connection to the chameleon in that they are masters of camouflage and illusion. This colouring panel lends itself to very spontaneous approach and no colours are suggested other than possibly a blue or aqua background for the water, which will highlight other bright colour use of complementary opposites.

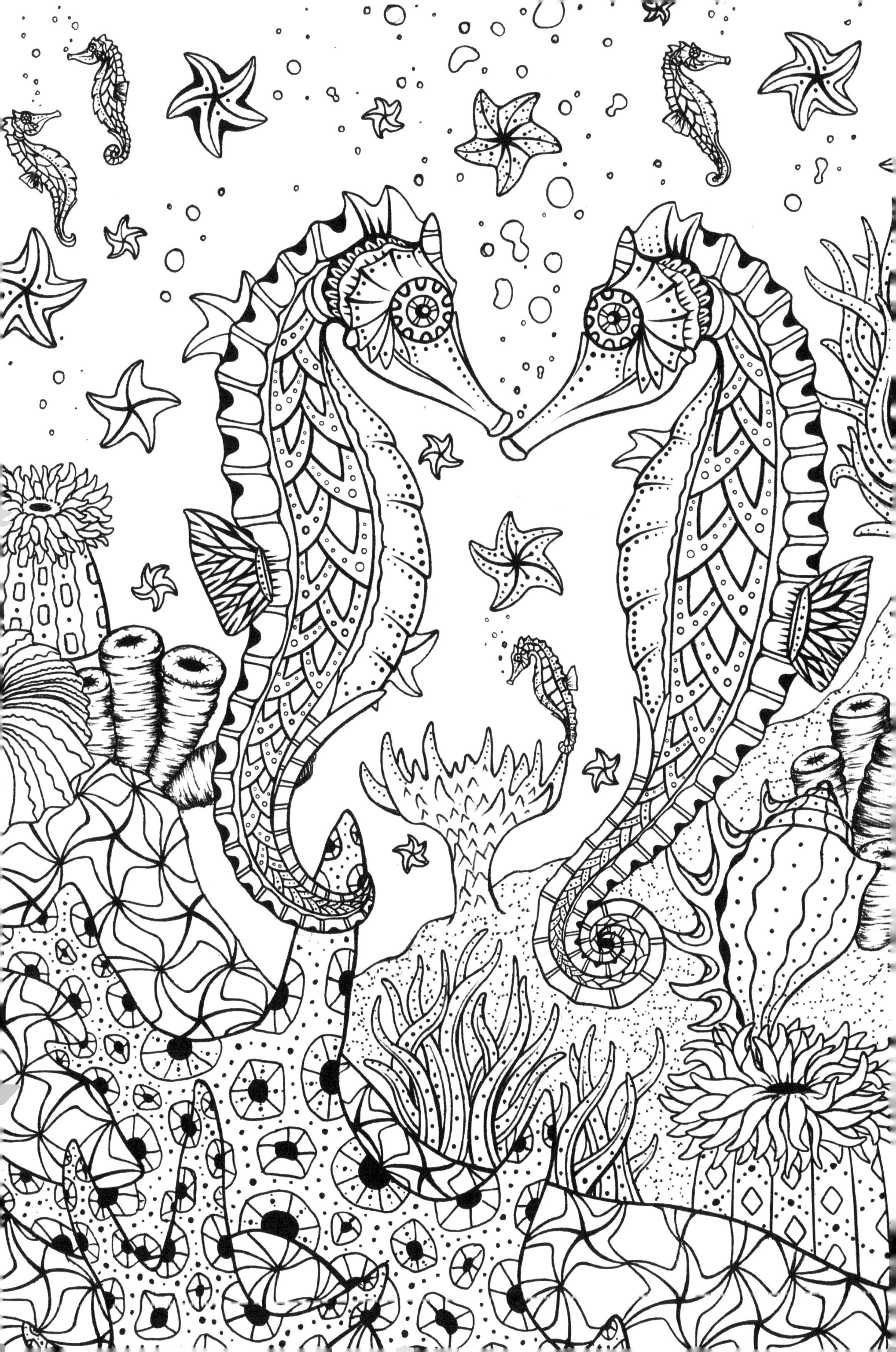

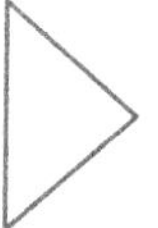

Lizards relate to the power of dreaming, to creativity and sensitivity to the very vibrations and rhythms of life. The lizard totem denotes insight, the power of perception and the very vision of life and psychic impressions. The gecko often appears at key times to remind us to pay attention to our dreams and visions, or that a special window of creative opportunities may be open to us at present or in the immediate future. The gecko totem is useful in times of personal transformation that result from new visionary insights and creative potential awakening. They represent a fertile transition into new dimensions of potential and growth. This totem reminds us what we are connected to and even attached to, may need to be let go or given up in the regeneration of the creative process, or in the context of greater life cycles. Lizards in general can relate to detachment from our surrounding, yet at the same time reminding us to be attentive or sensitive to the pulsating potential of opportunities that present themselves. This teaches us a great deal about detachment, objectivity, integrity and inner strength.

This image involves cactus flowers in the outer section. Colour freely and bold complimentary colours would suit well. Alternatively match colours for the gecko like greens, turquoise and electric blue with complimentary colours in the outer sections of your art pieces. Yellows, oranges and greens would also work well in the cactus flowers.

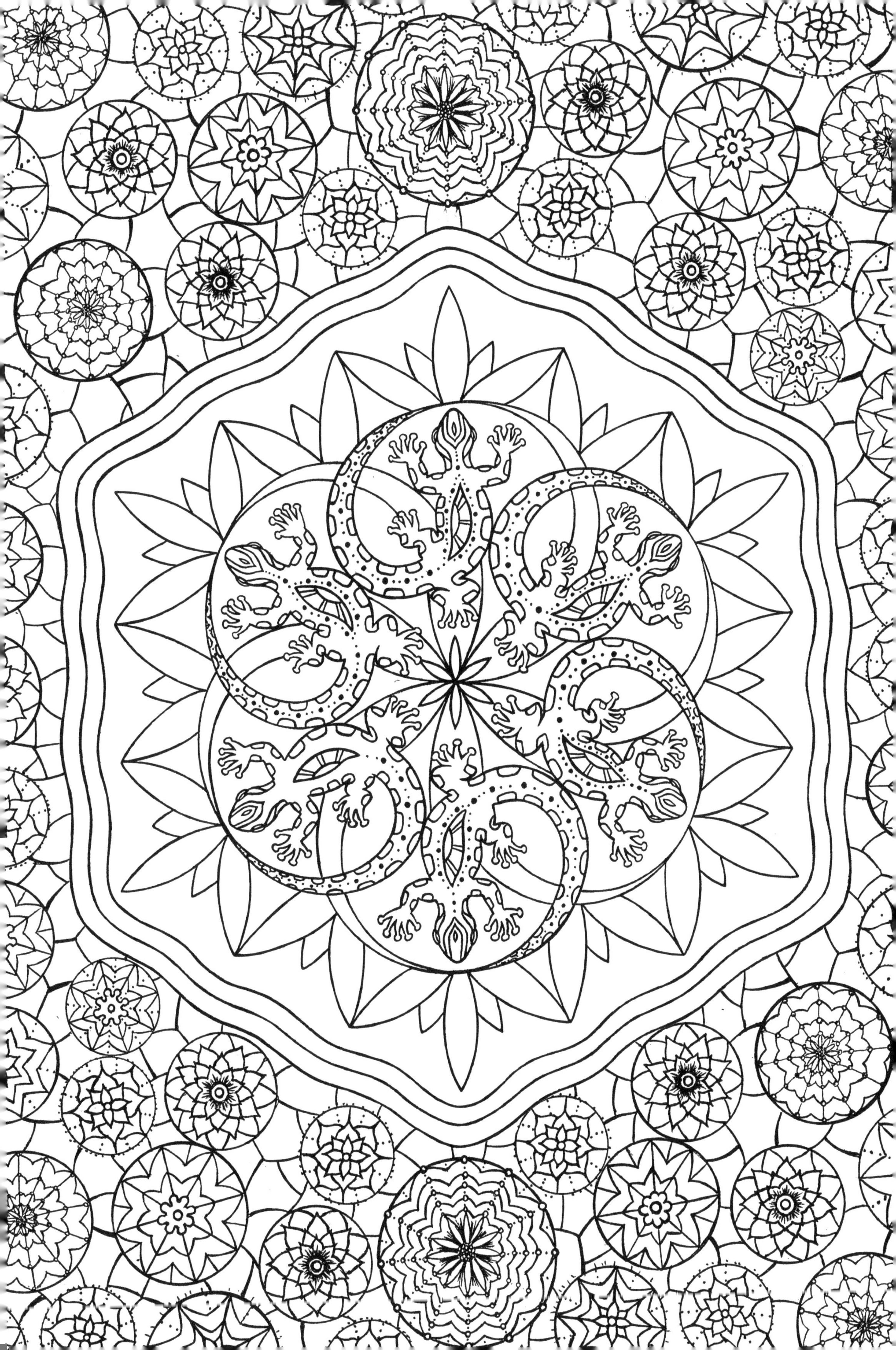

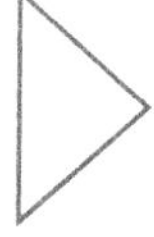

This lotus-based nature mandala incorporates water, leaves and flowers. The design was all hand-drawn without the use of a compass to give it a more organic and stylised feel. The image is dynamic, pulsating and vibrantly alive. It contains many elements with great potential for creative journeying and a transpersonal colouring experience. There is an inner and outer effect for example, when concentrating on the inner centre of radiating lotuses. There is a balance of aerial view and lateral expansion also, which is very growth enhancing and good for abundance and encouraging new growth or new beginnings into our life. The interlaced graphic elements are merely for a stylistic approach and give the design a certain timelessness or endless appeal. This design has a very meditative or potentially remedial effect on the mind. The lotus represents new life and abundance in golds, saffron and yellow hues. In relation to aspiration, new potential emerging and gentle creative energies, try soft pinks and pink-violet.

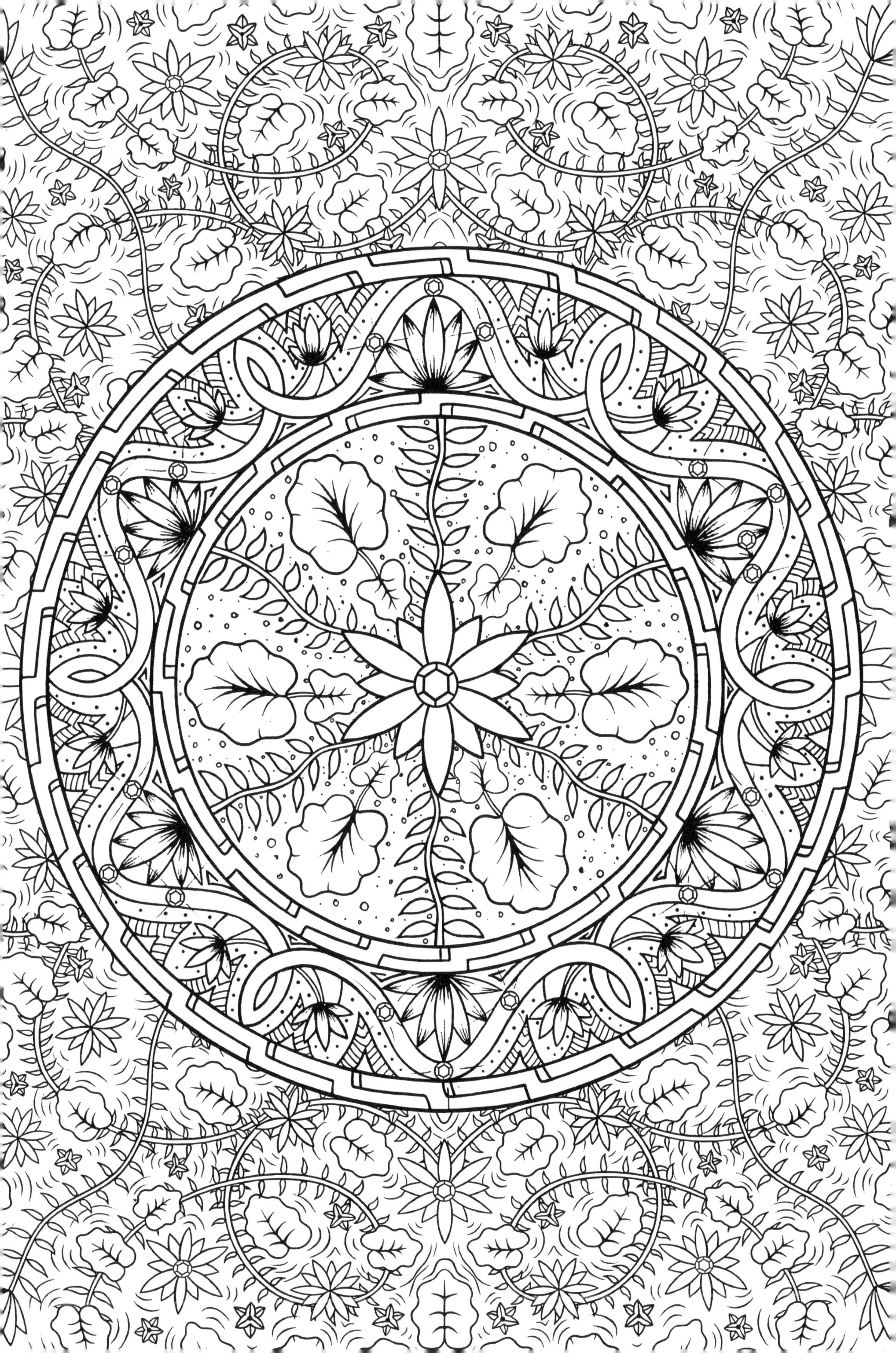

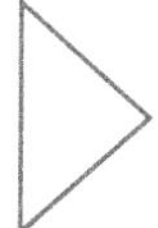

This colour panel is created in light of the spring call and new-found potential of the forrest wren. The wren teaches us to be light-hearted in our endeavours, yet at the same time to be determined and resourceful and to be appreciative of all that life has to offer. Wrens relate to heightened alertness and new dimensions of life energy opening up or coming into our life. They denote boldness, vibrancy and effervescence. Vibrant spring colours would be good, or you could try complementary colours for the bird and colour the tree and foliage at the bottom in greens and browns to balance or ground the use of otherwise bold and striking colours like indigo and gold, violet and yellow, or bright blue and orange. The flowers and fruits can then be added last to complement and bring balance once other colours are set in. Otherwise, start with the flowers first and then build complimentary and balancing colours with the other elements one by one. The bird will look more dynamic either in striking colours or in bright colours with areas possibly shaded to white. For a colour example see Fig. 8 in the colour section at the start of the book.

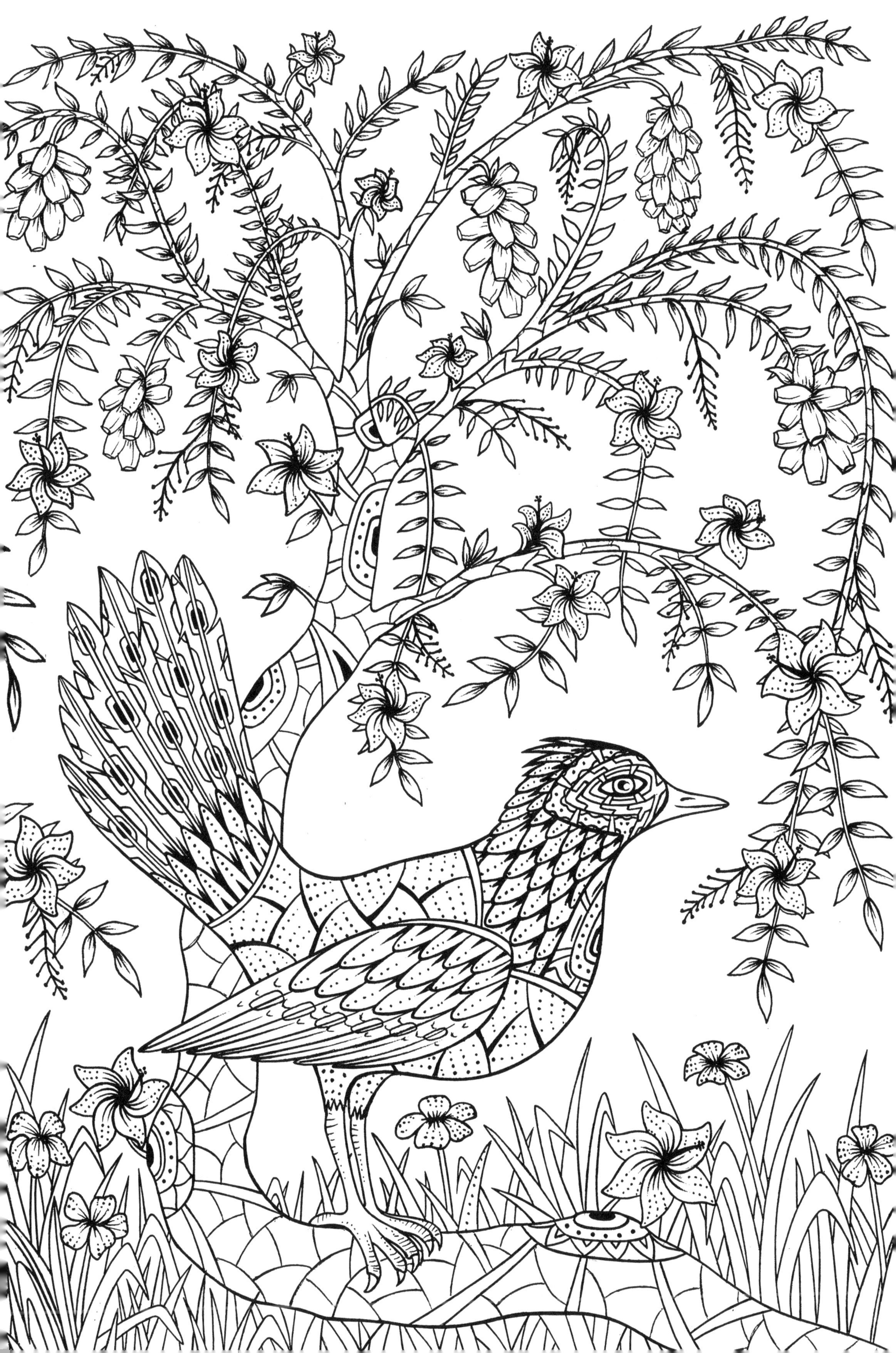

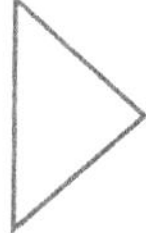

Cats are associated with many totemic values from the integrity and impeccability of the jaguar, to the sensitivity and passion of the tiger, or the regality and pride of the lion. The cats here represent refined sensitivity to the flux and transformation of life, with the butterflies denoting the flow of life forces and more specifically, the actual transmutation of life forces. The cats can be coloured as lions, panthers or even leopards or jaguars with spots or camouflaged markings. You may decide to add extra glyphs or stylised markings to the existing line art to make the design more detailed or appealing for a larger colouring panel. Simply draw first in pencils and then ink in once you have achieved the desired effect. Also, refer to the animal totem section at the back of the book for colours and extra input on totemic qualities.

This panel has a balance of masculine and feminine energies and is good for awakening courage of the heart, refined sensitivity and personal empowerment. The leaves around the outside could be green palm leaves to balance the other colours, or they could be flocks of butterfly wings for a more dynamic or transformative effect. Violets, purples, greens, burgundies and pinks are all well suited, or even try any of these hues will complimentary aquas or golds.

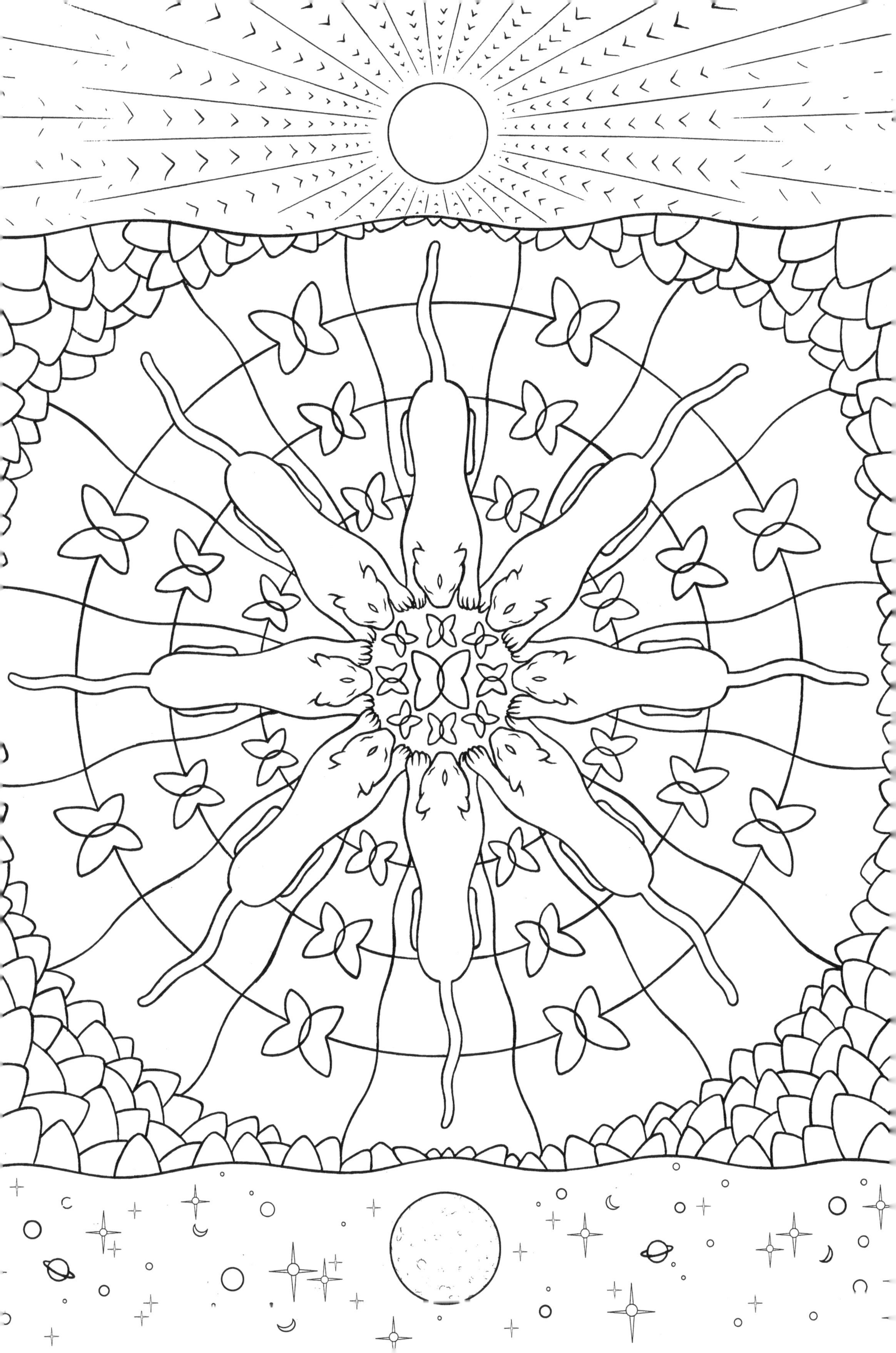

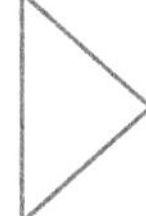

The Symbolism in this image conveys the awakening of creative power. Inspiration and creative potential go hand-in-hand, and in this light the warm and vibrant tones of the morning sun symbolise new beginnings and the activation of new-found creative power. Jaguars and leopards relate to the spirit of integrity and reclaiming our personal power. They also relate to refined sensitivity, especially to the power of sound and keen awareness to subtle vibrations. Working with them in artwork symbolises new dimensions of potential opening up. Snakes are also associated with personal power and transformation. Here the coiled rainbow coloured serpent symbolises the very cycle of creation and is held sacred for centuries among the indigenous people of Australia. Alternatively the snake can be coloured in yellow, golds, orange and violet tones.

The lotuses here symbolise the unfolding of creative potential and being open to the awakening of light and greater wisdom. They can be coloured in violet, blues, pink and even gold and orange to symbolise joy and aspiration. The crystals represent the reflection of light and glory of colour, through which they act as a prism or magnifier of the very power of colour. Colour these as you see fit and maybe personalise them in line with a favourite gem or crystal. The Inner Earth is featured here in association with grounded power and new aspiration being awakened and made fertile for growth. Colouring is often done best with a balance of colours from nature as well as an understanding of principles relating totems and fundamental colour symbolism. For more insights on colouring see the coloured example (Fig. 6 and refer to Masterclass 8).

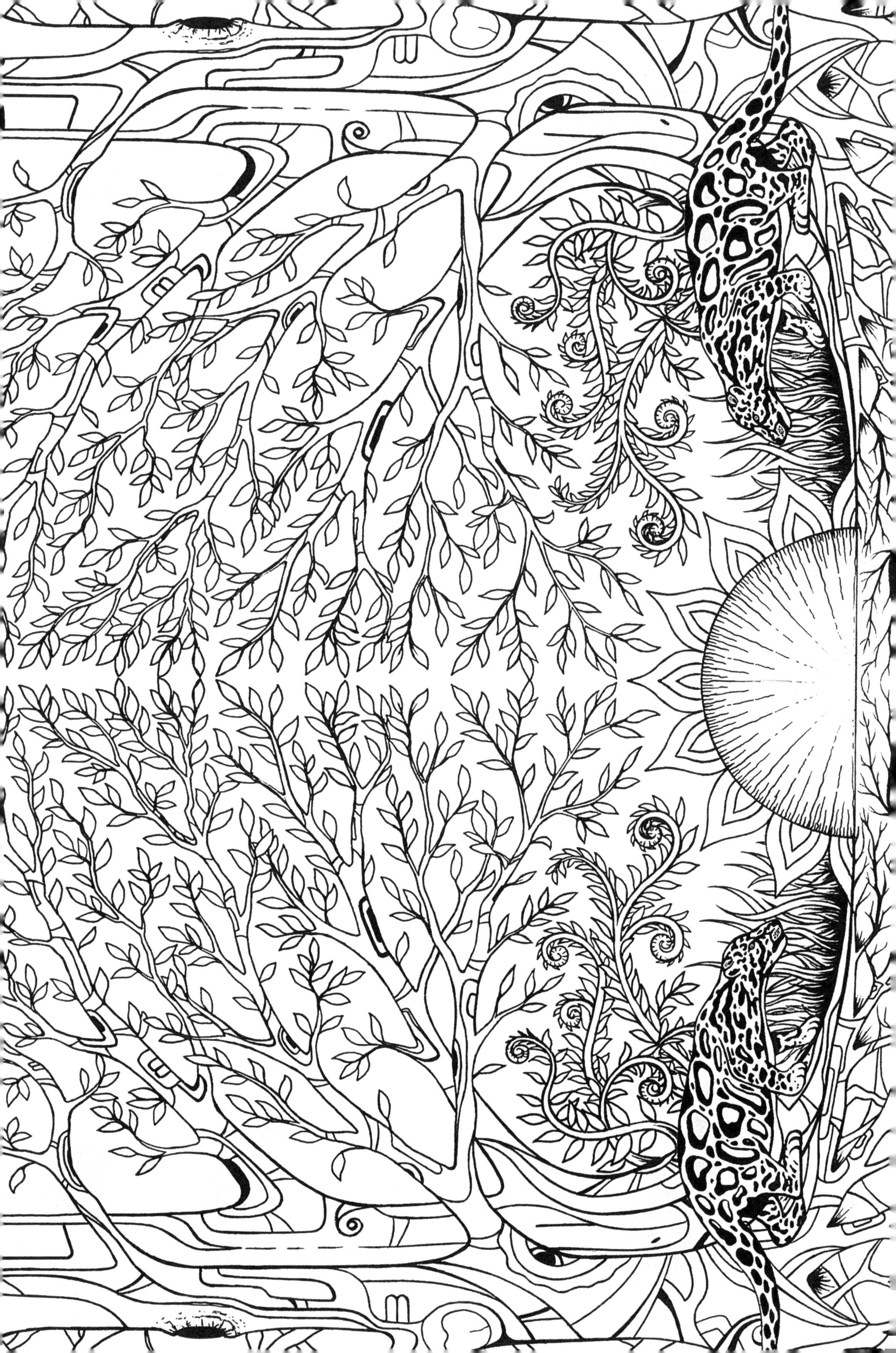

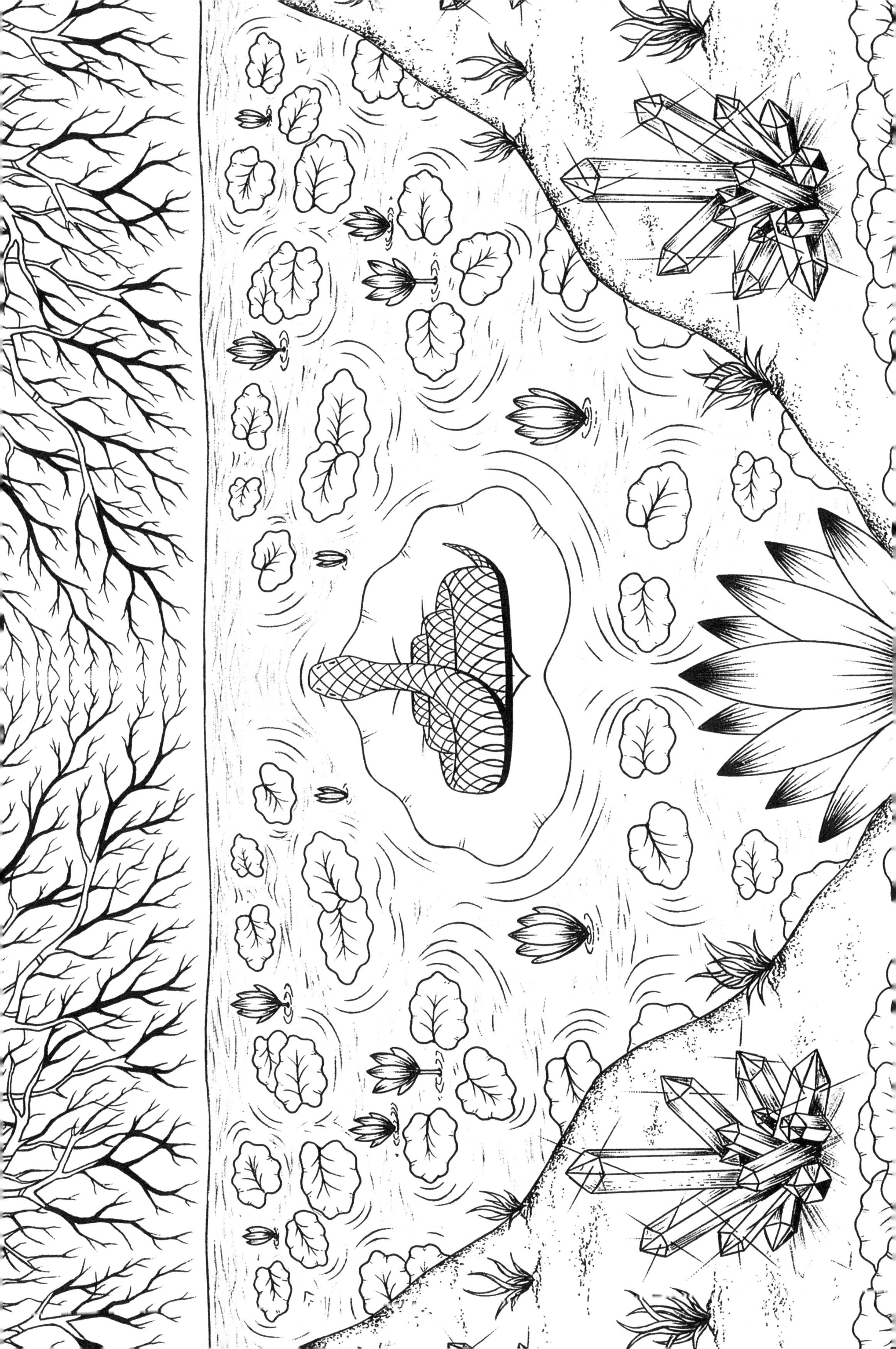

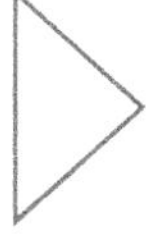

This mandala panel incorporates the four directions of space and symbols of nature such as birds, water and lotuses. The lotus symbol promotes an abundance of creative energies as it is a shape portraying freedom and expansion. It is a symbol of wealth and abundance and is held sacred among many ancient and modern cultures. The colour yellow is good for creating abundance and expansive potential in artwork (or any colour that you feel relates to abundance for you personally). Colour the 4 directional gateway sections in complementary opposites like red and blue, green and yellow, or choose two complementary opposites - one for left and right and another for above and below. Heavier or darker colours are best suited for left side and bottom section for balance. The birds can be doves for peace and tranquillity, or they may be hawks for perception and insight, ravens for mystery and magic, or eagles for wisdom and perfection. So choose colours according to what the birds chosen may best represent, or be most effective to you, as after all it is your personal colour space to represent yourself.

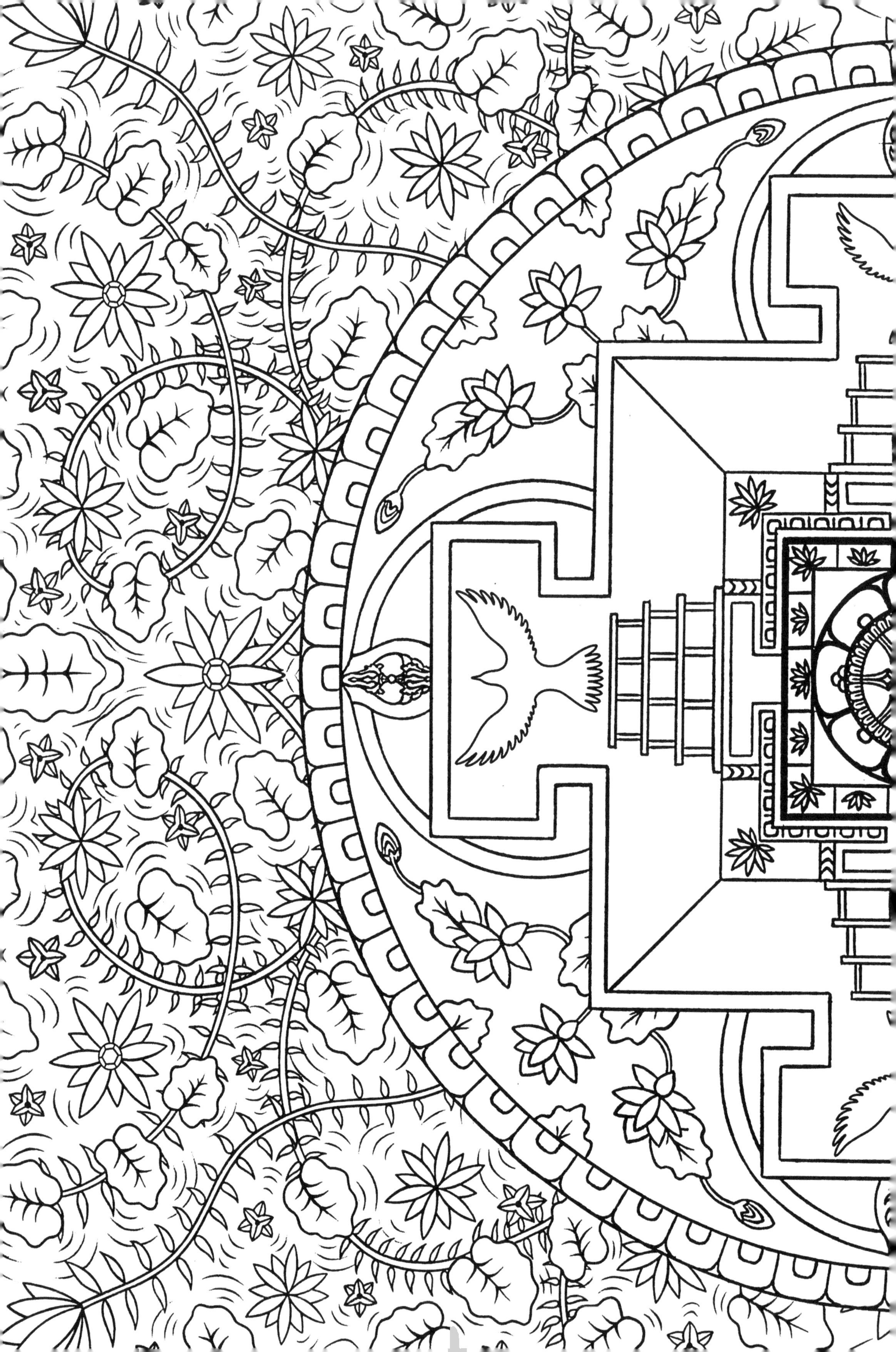

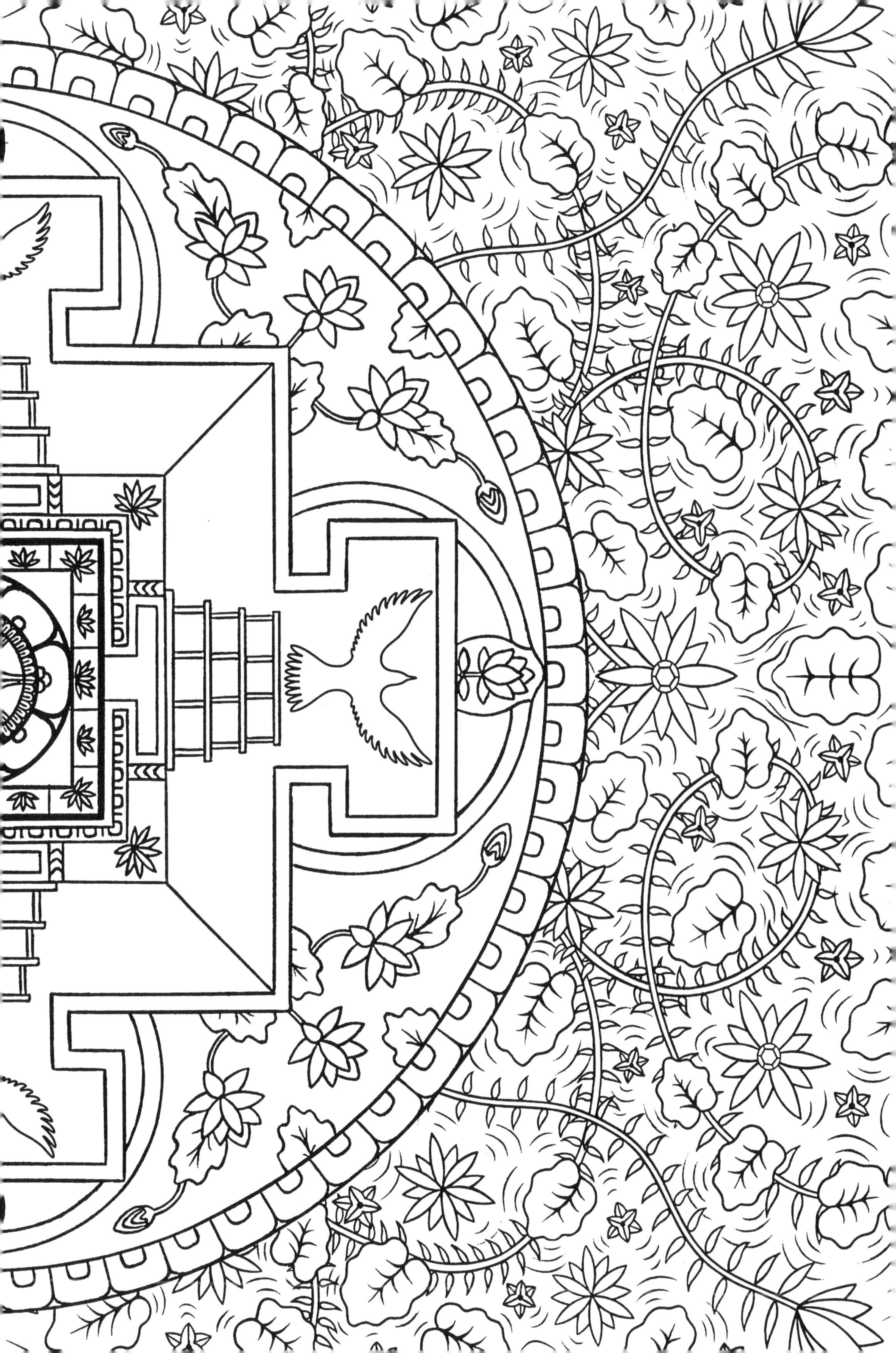

Animal Totem Qualities and Colours for Spatial Directions

Colours have been used for qualitative association by many cosmological systems and cultural traditions for centuries. When deciding to work more specifically with a design incorporating certain colours, symbols or animal totems, a more impactful and transpersonal experience can be attained. The image below shows one example for how animal totems could be used or associated with the 8 directions of space. Many variations could be created, depending on the individual creative purpose of the design or artwork. A personal mandala with your favourite animals totems for example, may be represented more artistically in terms of animals chosen and combined colours. A cultural design relating to the four directions however may be more intentionally focused in its syntax. It may call for a limited or somewhat narrower selection of animals chosen, based on the designs utilitarian purpose or need for certain attributal qualities.

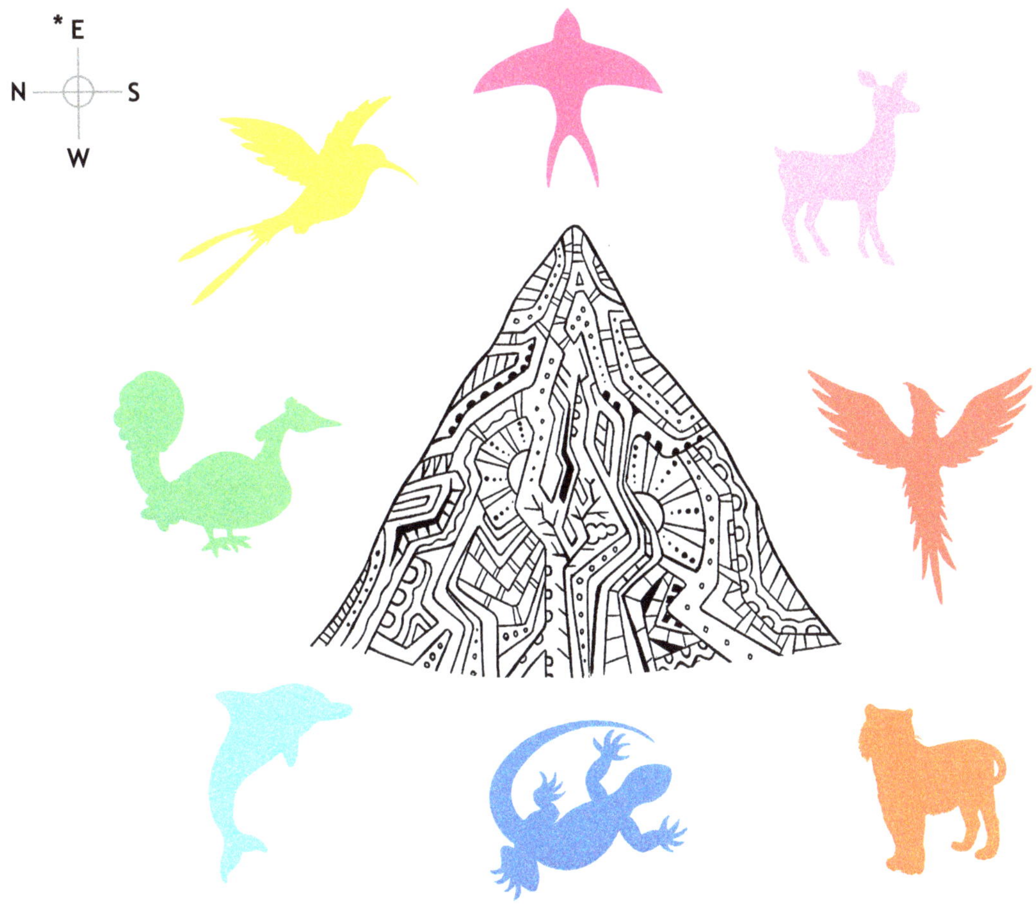

The example above shows animals associated with the 8 directions of space in the southern hemisphere. The one major difference is that the passage of the sun in the southern hemisphere is around to the north, whereas in the northern hemisphere it is around to the south. This association is a balance between esoteric and exoteric models, by where the animals chosen are still largely congruent with the passage of the sun in the northern hemisphere also. The image here is merely for symbolic purposes, with no degree or artistic effort or graphic stylisation being applied.

The swift here at the Eastern Gate represents the warming and enlivening energies released by the new dawn. By contrast in colour and symbolism, the lizard (The Western Gate) represents here the cool night time, stillness and the capacity to dream. In The North we have the Peacock, associated with preservation, fertility and majesty. The Phoenix, by contrast in colour, represents the transformative power of the South. Other associations are more bridging energetics, like the deer for refined sensitivity (Southeast), Tiger for courage and passion (Southwest), Dolphin for adaptability and the breath of life (Northwest). The Hummingbird is here associated with the Northeast as the lightest and most subtle of the directions and relates to the principles of joy and abundance. It cyclically bridges back with the energetic qualities of the swift totem.

* In Mandalas and Eastern Traditions East is often represented at the top different to map directions.

Masterclass 7: Animal Totem Colours and Symbolism

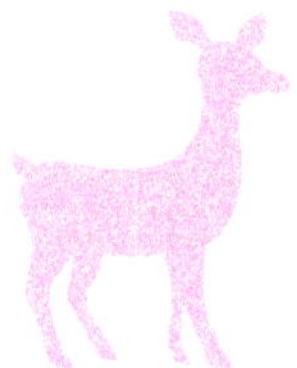

The **Deer** symbolises innocence, gentleness and purity. It is associated with the energies of the Moon and feminine attunement to Mother Nature's rhythms. The deer's gentleness helps heal hurt emotions and the wounded hearts and minds of those lost or confused. Colouring ideally in white or pink and pastel orange for refined sensitivity.

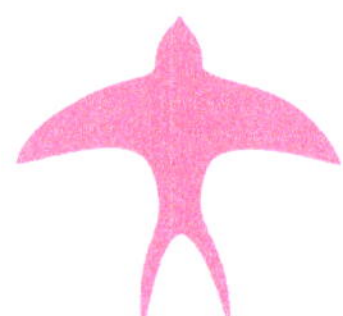

The **Swift** or **Swallow** relates to similar energy dynamics and to the pink-violet and violet hues. Swifts represent harmony within restrictions of the outer world, to spreading our wings, agility and the freedom of flight. The swallow represents welcoming energies, peace and preservation, relating to the turquoise or aqua hues.

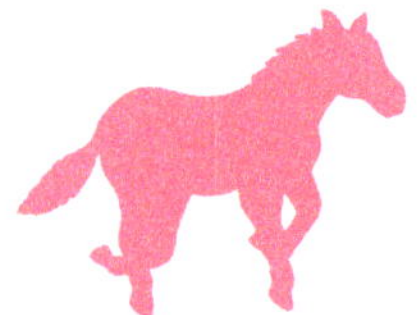

The **Horse** is a symbol of power and vitality. When associated with the sun, its appropriate colours are magenta and red. It can also embody more feminine qualities like allure and charm, which relates to Venus (white). When relating to the refinement of power, desire or sensuality, suggested colours are violet or pastel orange.

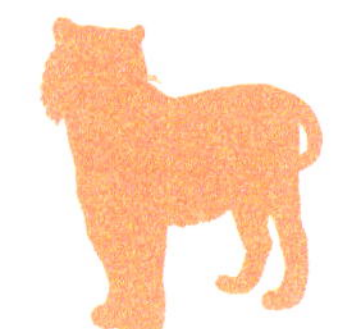

The **Tiger** symbolises passion and refined sensuality. Tigers display great motherly devotion. In the Indian tradition they are the vehicle of many goddesses and feminine deities and represent feline power and ferocity. They convey courage of the heart and the balancing of personal power. It is strongly tied with the colour orange and to burgundy or deep pinks/magentas with refining deeper desires.

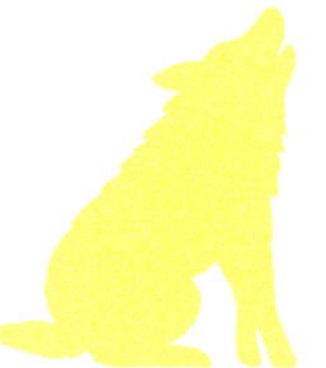

The **Coyote** signifies balance between wisdom and playfulness and is useful in awakening the magic and mystery of childlike characteristics. A trickster that loves fun, the coyote brings about simplicity and trust fostering a new visionary perspective. It helps rekindle a re-awakening of humour and intellect in balanced proportions. It relates well to the colour yellow, golds and golden-orange.

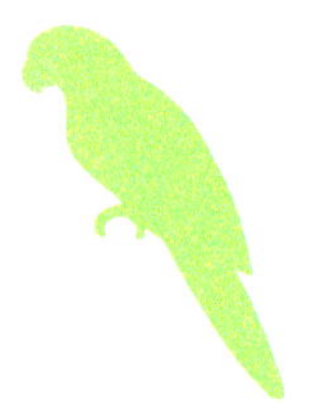

The **Parrot** is symbolic of love, romance and sensuality. Conveying freedom of growth and expression it is connected to the fertility of nature. It is associated with the energies of the goddess, and with rainbow colours with the planet Venus. Further qualities associated with the parrot are charm, affection and playfulness. Parrots are associated with the god or goddess of love in many traditions and folklore.

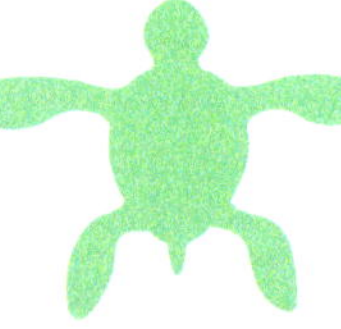

The **Turtle** is associated with the earth and water elements and a variety of colours depending on its syntax or image depiction. Black or blue for wealth potential and abundance forming. With the preservational energies of motherhood and fertile waters of life (grounding it to the earth) relates to jade green and aqua colours. Turtles have had much older and deeper cosmic symbolism through the ages.

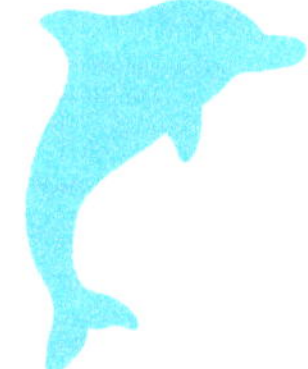

The **Dolphin** conveys the power of breath and sound, relating to communication, expression and emotional balance. They have a balanced dynamic between air and water, representing innocence and freedom. The dolphin is a calming totem tuned into the universal flow of life. Indigo, mid-blue and aqua tones are appropriate colours. It is a great totem to work with to help people find space to play.

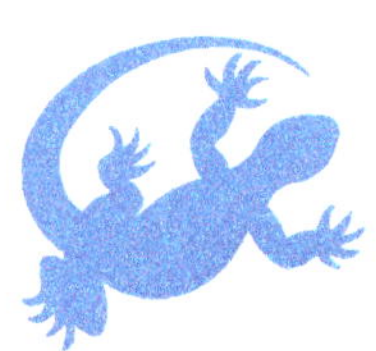

The **Lizard** represents intuitive vision and subtle perception, symbolising the balance between the waking and dreaming states of cognitive perception. It can provide a profound connection to the Dreamtime and is a valuable totem helping to bridge the conscious and subconscious mind, bringing foresight and vision. Main colours are indigo and electric blues, yet aqua colours are also well suited to this totem.

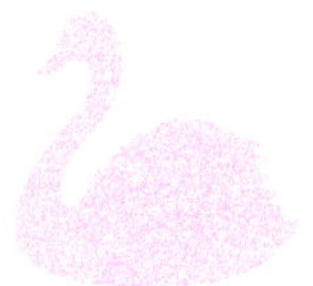

The **Swan** relates to refined qualities such as elegance, grace, harmony and purity. It is used to symbolise self-refinement and perfection. For transformation through self refinement, intuition, pure or refined knowledge it is aligned with the pink and violet hues. With water energies and purity it also relates to soft pastel blues and white.

The **Butterfly** signifies transformation of the life force from one stage to the next. A central image in the mandala, it reveals how the power of creation is transmuted. Representing freedom and new beginnings in the journey of life, its preferred colours are hot-pink and violet. Soft yellow and pastel hues can represent joy and freedom.

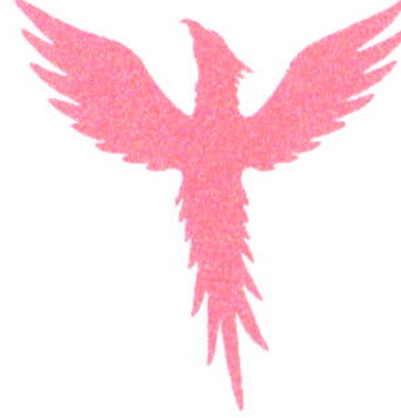

The **Phoenix** represents vitality and the transmutation of life energy relating to magenta tones. When symbolising the manifested form of power (transformation) its colour is slightly more violet than red, conveying balanced, power and completion. A good totem for manifesting and externalising creative power with the red hue.

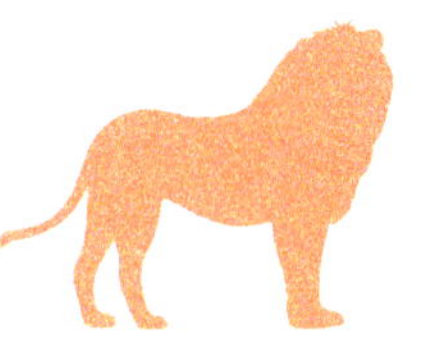

The **Lion** conveys coming into one's own power. It is dignified, regal and strong, playing out a balance between the sun and moon. Lions symbolise courage and the expression of a non-domineering power, relating well to orange and yellow. Lions also have a connection to kingship, the ego and pride. They are good totems to work with if the ego or sense of self is weak, or the individual is timid or in need of courage.

The **Hummingbird** symbolises joy and new beginnings and is great when light expansive energies are needed. It relates well to the complementary colours yellow and violet. As totems for transformation and the change from one state of creation to another, this totem can be helpful for moving through creative blocks and personal emotional hurdles. Colouring in variegated colours can be useful in this regard.

The **Bee** represents fertility, creativity and the alchemical process. Intimately connected with the pollination process and the blossoming of life. It is also associated with femininity, sensuality and mystical wisdom. Shown in lime green and yellow tones depicting here the energies of spring and fertility. This colour is intricately connected with new beginnings and new life, as we see with new shoots in the plant kingdom.

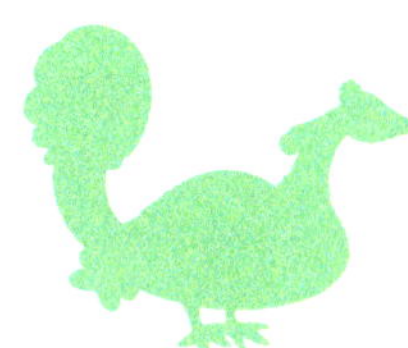

Peacocks relate to the majesty of creation and are held sacred amongst many cultural traditions. They symbolise majestic expression, glory, grace and favour. Its combined energetics can be represented by the balancing green hue, yet it can be used to represent qualities of the blue and blu-violet hues.

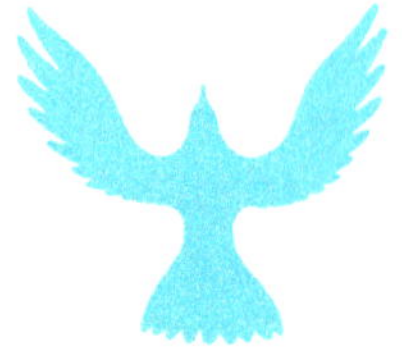

The **Dove** is universally associated with hope and peace. It suggests purity, unity, refinement and higher virtues. As a messenger of peace it is associated with the water element and pure emotions. Invoking new life, the dove relates to blue for peace, light violet for refinement and harmony, and white for purity. The dove's connection with hope also relates to the soft or mid-blue hues.

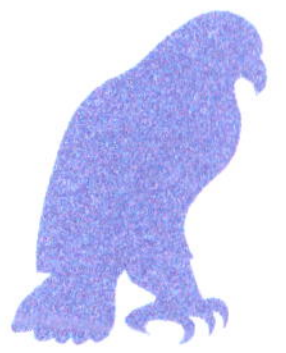

Hawks are associated with the principles of insight, foresight and greater visionary capacity. Hawks are often used to depict messengers of the heavens, gods or higher celestial realms. They are protective talismans for many and relate to varying colours depending on image depiction. Indigo for insight and revelation and gold for illuminated wisdom and the ability to have expanded awareness or vision.

Masterclass 8: Defining Colour Qualities &Tonal Variations

The following colour guide explains the symbolic qualities associated with individual colours. Using and combining colours in thoughtful and intentional ways undoubtedly enhances the artwork.

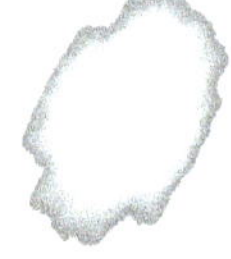

White

White symbolises liberation and collective energy of the highest potential. It is associated with purity and the feminine planets Venus and the Moon, along with their associated element 'water'. White helps purify and pacify the emotions. White is often used to provide contrast and to bridge or shade other colours through lightening or softening their tonality. White sections in nature panels give space and heighten the energetic potential of other colours.

Violet

Violet is associated with harmony when neutral or slightly warm in hue. As it approaches purple, it becomes more inert, becoming passive as deep purple, which relates to the void, representing energy returning to its origin or source. In its mid-tones, violet conveys neutrality and its brighter shades, higher transformation. Soft pastel violet is associated with tranquillity and equilibrium. This is a unique combination of the coming together of two opposite energies (red and blue). Violet works well for twilight skies in nature panels and for flowers, colourful birds, fish, corals and starfish.

Magenta

Magenta represents the passion and vitality of the creative force (red) merged with the white and violet rays. It signifies aspiration. In mandalas it is used to evoke the goddess, for colouring lotuses and to depict creative energies unfolding. Magenta is commonly used to colour triangles and the Sun. It is a great colour to use in nature panels in place of red, or in an image where red may clash with other colours. Similar to hot-pink it works well for undersea colouring of corals, for flowers and early morning rising sun.

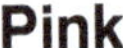

Pink

Pink has a calming and harmonising effect on the emotions. It promotes aspiration and helps refine deeper creative urges, as it is technically a predominance of pacifying white with a touch of red. Pink can symbolise creativity manifesting gently and the potential for refined sensitivity. In mandalas, pink is usually for gentle feminine energies and used for colouring auspicious goddesses, abundance manifesting and lotus or flower images. It can also represent the feminine aspect of the morning Sun associated with inspiration, the Sun and Moon, or Mars and Venus merged in unison. It represents male and female balance, yet is considered to be predominantly of feminine attributes. Like magenta, it works well, and is good when needing to bring soft and sensitive qualities into an image, for morning or twilight sky's, birds and flowers. Very effective as a complementary opposite with greens and aqua tones

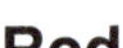

Red

Red is associated with desire, fertility and manifestation. In cosmology it represents the fire element and dynamic attributes of creation. Slightly cool red relates to passion, deep red to lust, or integration of sensuality and deeper desire. In association with astrological influences however, red harnesses the qualities of masculine planets like Mars and the Sun (Mars as fire red and magenta for the Sun). It is an appropriate colour for triangles, fan shapes, crescents and flames. Red can be used for passion in flowers. It represents transformation, though not essentially positive in this regard. It is great in burnt-red and cool red for defining some tree branches with complimentary greens, for orchids and flowers with yellow and orange and for bold contrast in birds and parrots.

Orange

Orange is used to show the gentle masculine or slightly feminine energies of the rising sun. Blended with golden yellows and pinks it represents a gentle creative force. Pastel orange with a predominance of white, as we see in the full moon, represents auspiciousness. Very soft pastel orange represents maternal and nurturing energies. Bright orange and red-orange relates more to inspiration moving towards desire. It starts to instigate Mars, the principles of externalisation and manifestation in the physical world. Softer pastels are great for adding softness to skies, refined sensitivity and bring nurturing qualities into an image. Burnt orange and deep orange tones are good for complementing other colours, for earthy scenes and some sky depictions. Orange also works well for detailing trees and for animals, birds and parrots.

Yellow

Yellow represents expansive qualities and is often used to colour the outer square or perimeter of a mandala. It is used in some cultural traditions to symbolise the earth element. However this is often an esoteric association, as yellow does not represent the fundamental qualities of Earth (i.e heavy, gross, coarse). It often works better as amber and earthy yellows or deep yellows which become brown for earthy nature scenes. In its saffron tone it represents joy, abundance, general wealth and good fortune. Great for birds, parrots, flowers and for contrasting and defining artwork when boldness and vibrancy is needed. Great as a contrasting complementary when used with all aquas, blues and violets.

Gold

Golden tones - pure gold (metallic) depicts the highest of vibrations. Relating to perfection and transcendence, it is used to emphasise shapes representing the highest virtues or most regal of qualities. It can be utilised for fine lines along with gold leafing in artwork or mandalas. Gold can also be used for majestic depictions, to represent royalty and kingship, as we see in crests and crowns. It is considered masculine, bold and defining and good for defining outer lines. You can emboss flowers and any stylised lines in artwork with gold for an expensive or regal effect. Gold in the colour wheel (Fig. 2) can be used in place of metallic gold and suits spring flowers and sunrises.

Lime

Lime is used to invoke fertile and activating life-giving energies. It relates to new growth and the vitality of spring. Lime can be used in gardens, or the outer square of a mandala for active and communicative life energies, where it conveys invigorating qualities. Use sparingly, as lime has a vitalising and stimulating effect and too much can be overpowering in artwork. It complements well with violets, blues and aqua, yet clashes with red and somewhat with red-orange.

Green

Green is somewhat linked to lime. Green fosters communication, preservation and exchange. It reflects properties such as growth and fertility. As vibrant mid-green it depicts interconnection, with the cooler emerald or blue-green shades conveying calmness or balance. Green is often used to signify the air element and the equalising attribute of nature, as it can be either warm as lime green (slightly active) or cool as emerald or aqua-green (slightly passive). It suits detailing leaves, grass and foliage, yet can also be used for many animals and nature settings. Parrots relate well to green and some lizards such as geckos and chameleons. Great for using in various shades in forest settings and contrasts well with browns, blues, aqua and violet.

Aqua

Effective when working with higher expression of the emotions, for communicative energies in general and pacifying intense emotions. It helps calm or soothe more intense aspects or our self-expressive capacity. Great for water settings and animals that depict peaceful and playful energies like the dolphin, otter and some birds like parrots and even falcons and hawks.

Aqua-greens are good for the air element and represent the principles of intercommunion and sustenance. They work well with contrasting colours like gold, amber and orange when it suits the artwork and story or expression being defined or created. They can be used instead of cyan blue or true green if they better suit for complementary effects as this is technically a bridging hue between these two colours. Can be used in forest setting and tropical scenes to great effect and for subtle detailing in foliage, leaves and flowers.

Aqua-blue means more blue than green. This hue can relate to the water element and the flow of our emotions and creative expression. Turquoise fosters freedom of artistic expression and refined sensitivity. It suits the elements of air and water. Aqua colours are favoured by artists for these reasons and can work well with indigo, violet and light brown or tan colours. They also compliment black and can be used to lighten up or take the edge off of black's otherwise heavy or restrictive qualities. Great for parrots, lizards, water and sky settings and for contrasting yellow and gold-orange.

Blue

Blue in its lighter tones is similar to aqua and can be used in nature settings and mandalas to represent gentle passive or peaceful qualities. It is used symbolically to represent the air element as light to mid pastel blue, which promote openness and expansiveness. Blue relates to gentle and refined expression of energies and relates well to peaceful birds like parrots and dove. It also relates to the sky from light through to mid blue, which can also be used to symbolise the ocean, as ocean water reflects the blue of sky. As it starts to move toward warm blue or deep blue its energetic attributes change somewhat. Here we start to get qualities suitable for deep oceans or the night sky as with the indigo hue.

Indigo

This hue is half way between blue and purple, yet more on the blue side and considered a warm blue by some. Indigo relates to the principles of insight, inner wisdom and revelation. It can be used to represent depth in an image and for ocean and night sky settings. It also relates to the principles of structure and mental integration. It compliments well with aqua, green, yellow and orange hues. Indigo represents purposefulness and structural integrity and is utilised when defining boundaries. The most invigorating of the blue tones when not too dark, relating to creative vision in life. In its deeper tones it encourages insight into life's more contemplative mysteries.

Purple

Somewhere between indigo and violet, purple is considered closer in energetic qualities and effect to indigo. Purple is neutral to cool and somewhat negating in effect. It is good for creating depth in an image and defining boundaries. It relates to the integration of opposites like the meeting of red and blue. It can be used in night depictions and deep sea or for colourful birds, flowers, gems and minerals and to add depth to skies. Deep purple has similar qualities to deep blue.

Deep Blue

Blue is neutral, passive in its mid-tones, yet as it starts to become darker it relates more directly to passiveness and inertia. This colour can be depressive in large amount or environments as it harnesses the limiting and retarding energies of Saturn. In traditional sacred art, dark blue is often used to represent the qualities of inertia, structure and contraction. Deep blue also relates to withdrawal, or receding and connecting with the life source vibration. It represents creativity taking form, the gestation or womb state of creation in this regard.

Black

Black defines the light and all other colours. It is used in mandalas for border designs and boundaries, representing structure. It represents qualities like negation, subtraction and devolution. It is also associated with the heavy and gross qualities of the earth element. Black can be used to depict negative or wrathful energies, or inertia and darkness in general. Not truely considered a colour, yet used more for its energy-negating effects or for defining a foundation.

Black can also work effectively to create small null spaces or void in sections of artwork as well as for containing the artwork. It can also represent fear and may be used in small carefully placed areas in artwork when moving through difficult personal junctures, or emotions like grief or sorrow. It can also be useful when working with the shadow side of the psyche. It represents the mysterious, the limited and the unknown.

Grey

In its mid smoky colour, grey is traditionally used in mandalas to depict the element 'ether'. In its light smoky tones it is also associated with the air element, to unseen, veiled or invisible energies. Used in the mandala it emphasises both beauty and perfection as neutral or slightly cool greys. Grey can also be seen as a shade of black and when shading can be used as per black in its darker shades.

Blue-greys can represent unmanifest forms, the conception of form, or an element of turbulent or abrupt change, as in the colour of storm clouds. Lighter blue-greys can be used for a complimentary effect, or for areas or designs that call for gentle contraction or undefined qualities manifesting, or that are in a state of flux. They provide somewhat relaxing or soothing effects. Not by themselves though, yet better mixed with more vibrant greens, blues, violets or even yellows and golds.

Brown

Symbolises the earth element in its most basic association, especially dark browns which represent heavy, static or solid foundational energies in artwork. Brown can be used effectively in colouring panels, yet with caution as it can get muddy or dirty depending on the design.

Red-browns are good for colouring squares, grounds and outer perimeters of drawings and designs. They mix well with yellow, orange or gold hues and even warm violets and pinks. They represent the principle of manifestation and become warmer with reds, pinks and violets added. More earthy, grounding and complimentary are deeper browns with golden browns or amber hues. These hues also work well with squares and triangular shapes and earthy animal totems like the ram, snake (earth snake), bull and horse. Also good for some earth minerals and crystals and for fruits, flowers, berries and native fauna.

Green-browns Great for nature scenes, providing they are not too dirty or muddy. Green browns and mid to light brown or tan colours are great for colouring any images that relate to nature, growth, or the principles of practicality and sustenance. They work well with other greens, aquas, blues and purple hues. Muddy browns and swampy tawny green-browns however represent wrathful energies of nature, like we see in the army-green colours.

Tawny green-browns are traditionally used to show negative and destructive energies of wrathful forces in sacred art. Relating to murky colours, such as a swamp it promotes turbulent or chaotic energies. These hues should generally be avoided unless in small amounts to create dramatic tension in an image or to divide a segment or area of a panel. They can alternatively work well with swamps, mud, trees and leaves and compliment well with aqua, blues and golden hues.

Masterclass 9: Colour Shading and Colour Tones

Colour shading is one of the most rewarding and effective skills to master and apply in our artwork. Colours are effectively light frequencies and by learning how to apply variation in colour shading and between specific hues of the color spectrum, our artwork becomes far more dynamic and visually alive. There are no set rules to colour shading so aim to experiment with complimentary colours and contrasting or supporting colours.

Colour shading also includes colour toning. For example; if we shade a medium or dark blue through to almost nothing we get light blues in the tonal gradient due to the underlying white paper. So shading may be employed to produce a variation in tone, where a heavy pencilling or laying down of pigment results in a gradation to a lighter version of the same hue or colour. This effect is great for creating three dimensional effects and for subtle shading on small objects to give a more dynamic or vibrant effect.

Colour tonation can be achieved by either shading mixed hues or tones, or by simply shading a colour inter-mixed with shaded black on the dark end and leaving white paper on the lighter end. Also, dark blues and indigo blues can be shaded with lighter cyan or sky blues for effects relative to these colours. Again experiment with adjoining colours and hues for example - red, orange and yellow. Another way for great effects is to miss one colour in the spectrum and then pick up the next two like: magenta, (miss red) and then use orange and yellow.

Shading also emphasises the movement of energies or colour and caters to a more dynamic emotive effect, especially with vibrant hues and bright or warm colours. Dark blue for example even when shaded is more static in effect, where as deep or dark blue shaded through to aqua or turquoise becomes balancing or neutral. If it was a warm indigo or ultramarine blue with turquoise, then it would have a slightly dynamic or vibrant effect overall when shaded, or in result of the combined final shading as an 'admixture'.

Dynamic and visually arresting effects can also be achieved by shading combinations of complimentary colours in regards to the colour qualities detailed on the former pages. Shading effects utilising complimentary opposites like blue and orange or yellow and violet can have a balancing effect in mandalas and imagery, especially when chosen to match image's elements or objects, or the overall subject matter. For example; violet and yellow used to colour imagery involving eagle or elk totems, or with expansive diagrams and crescent, teardrop, or dynamic elipse shapes.

Other points to note on shading and tonality are that in the very process of shading we are working with the emotional parts of the brain in terms of what we are visually creating or bringing into being. So this is an important part of shading with colours and bringing some kind or creative uniqueness or colour signature to our art pieces. Shading with black and grey tones has its own effects and is still effective on the emotional body and parts of the brain, yet more in a defining capacity and has more to do with base tonality rather than the subtle nuances of colour shading.

Always remember that colour is there to be freely experimented with, to have fun or to allow our self expressive capacity to become more multifaceted or mutlidimensional. A good deal of our skills to do with colour usage and colour shading are often mastered by free association and practicing until we achieve a pleasing or desired effect.

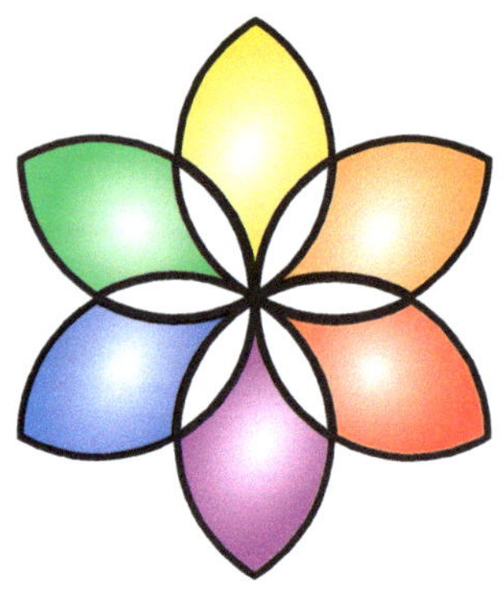

Complementary Colour Usage

Complementary colours can be used in many ways in our artwork, images and designs. The traditional approach might be to utilise complementary opposites, which works well when contrasting effects are needed. The use of complimentary opposite colours in artwork can also create balance in the left and right brain hemispheres. This brings scope for a whole range of beneficial and potentially remedial effects.

Also the term 'complementary' may apply to a colour that compliments another for a variety of reasons. A dusty and slightly muted pink for example complements purple and violet just as we see in a majestic sunset. Golden yellow may be employed to compliment its brother or sister hues of orange and red. So there are many ways to employ complementary colour usage with the potential for effect in mind.

In the spirit of creativity and to help further enliven your colouring journey, the following base colours are a guide for opposites and complementary effects :

Supporting Complementaries -

- Red, yellow and orange.
- Green, Indigo and violet.
- Purple, green and Aqua.
- Yellow, Turquoise and blue.

Complementary Opposites -

- Red and Green or Red and Blue.
- Orange and Blue or Orange and Purple.
- Yellow and Violet or Yellow and Blue.

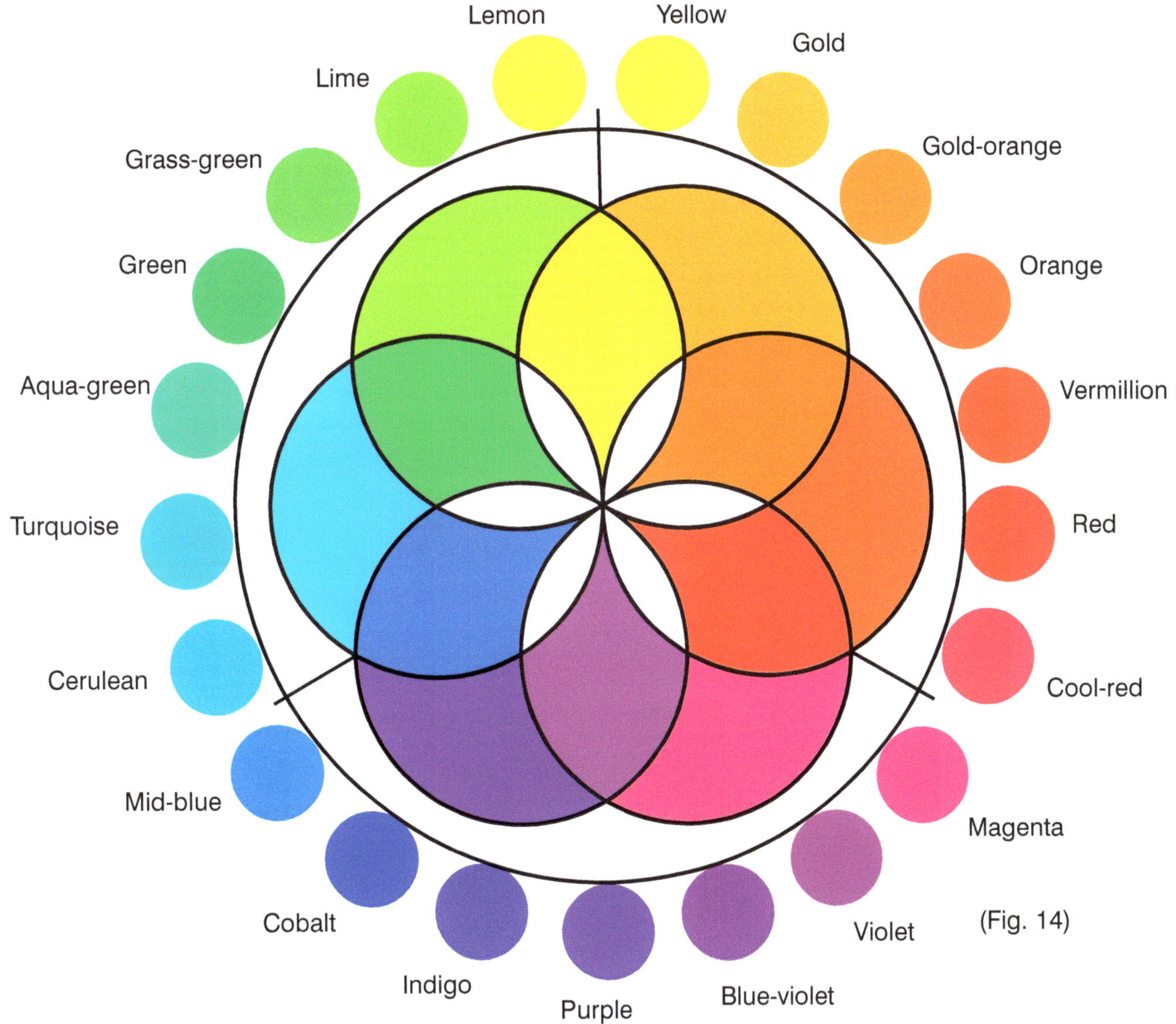

(Fig. 14)

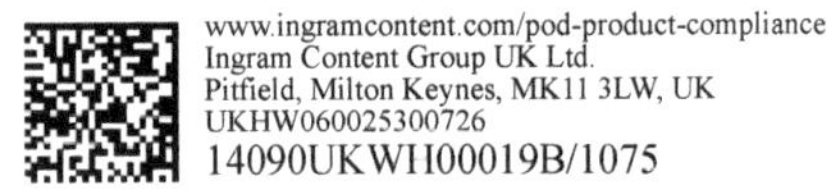

www.ingramcontent.com/pod-product-compliance
Ingram Content Group UK Ltd.
Pitfield, Milton Keynes, MK11 3LW, UK
UKHW060025300726
14090UKWH00019B/1075

9 780994 461926